COLLINS P[O...]

IRISH
FAMILY NAMES

John Grenham
Heraldic Illustrations by Myra Maguire

HarperCollins*Publishers*

HarperCollins Publishers
P.O. Box, Glasgow G4 0NB

First published 1997

Reprint 10 9 8 7 6 5 4 3 2 1 0

ISBN 0 00 472070 9

A catalogue record for this bookis available from The British Library

Printed and bound in Great Britain by
Caledonian International Book Manufacturing, Glasgow

Contents

Contents

Introduction

Although there is little that is not self-explanatory in the text, a little background on some of the items included with the accounts of individual families is necessary. First, the demographic data. The 1890 figures come from Matheson's *Special Report on Surnames in Ireland*, published in 1896. This is based on the state records of births for 1890, and gives details of the number of births recorded for each surname and, for some names, details of the areas in which the name is most commonly found. Only names with more than five births are included. Unfortunately there is no contemporary equivalent of Matheson, as yet. For the 1996 figures, then, I have had to rely on the telephone directories of Northern Ireland and the Republic of Ireland. Obviously these do not give details of the number of births, and the only way in which they can be compared with Matheson is in the relative rankings of the different names. Even here, though, there is necessarily some imprecision – a good 30% of telephone subscribers are ex-directory. Still, in the vast majority of cases there is a remarkable consistency between the 1890 and 1996 rankings, and it seems unlikely that a predisposition to keep your telephone number private runs in the family.

The principles used in choosing the areas of Ireland to which the families are related in the accompanying maps were, of necessity, flexible; the text describes change, evolution and migration, while the maps can provide only a stationery snapshot. So the areas chosen for the maps depend on the circumstances outlined in the text. In some cases these areas may be the counties in which births of the name were most numerous in 1890, in others the areas in which the name originated, in still others the territories in which the families became best known. In any case, it is important to realise that the broad generalities of a book such as this have only the most tangential connections with the particulars of any one family's genealogy. In other words, don't blame me if your ancestors didn't come from where I say the family originated!

Acknowledging here all the debts acquired in the course of compiling this book would be tedious, and embarrassing, but some few cannot be passed over in silence. Dr. Edward MacLysaght's *Irish Families* (Irish Academic Press, 1957), an extraordinary compendium of folklore and scholarship, is the founder of the genre, while Robert Bell's *The Book of Ulster Surnames* (Blackstaff Press, 1988) and Ida Grehan's *Irish Family Histories* (Roberts Rinehart, 1993) have both expanded and enriched its scope. In addition, many excellent local collections of histories have appeared recently, of which the most notable are *Family Names of County Cork* (Diarmuid O Murchadha, Glendale Press, 1985), *Family Names of Co. Wexford* (Hilary Murphy, Geography Publications, 1985) and 'Donegal Families' by Fergus Gillespie in *Donegal History and Society* (ed. Liam Ronyne, Geography Press, 1995). I also owe personal debts to the staff of both the Genealogical Office and the National Library of Ireland for their patience and good humour in the face of my repeated onslaughts. But my biggest debt, as ever, is to Breda, Doireann and Eoin, and to them goes my biggest thank you.

John Grenham
Dublin , 1997

Irish Emigrants and Immigrants

Prehistory

The first arrivals appear to have reached Ireland about 10,000 years ago from northern Britain, which at that point was still a peninsula of the European mainland. We know little of them; traces of their way of life remain principally in the north of the island and point to a life of hunting, fishing, migrating as the resources of the land dictated. But in reality, we know next to nothing about these people who inhabited Ireland for more than forty-five centuries.

Only with the coming of the Neolithic peoples, perhaps around 3500 BC, does our ignorance lessen a little. Because they were farmers, domesticating animals, sowing crops and using more sophisticated tools, we have evidence of a way of life and can begin to reconstruct some parts of their lives and culture. There are tantalizing glimpses of a complex, culturally rich society with elaborate beliefs and well-developed skills in metalworking, building, astronomy and trading. The civilization that produced the complex of megalithic tombs along the Boyne valley was self-evidently a powerful, well-organised hierarchy. But even these can only give glimpses of a lost history that lasted for more than twenty-five centuries.

The Celts

'Pre-history' is a very small figleaf for our ignorance. 'History' begins with the appearance of the invaders who have determined the character of Ireland for the last two millennia, the Celts. The earliest Celtic arrivals appear to have come *c.* 600 BC via what is now Scotland into eastern Ulster, and were known to later annallists as Cruithín, or Pretani or Picti. They were the ancestors of the tribes of

Dál Riada, which dominated north-eastern Ulster for over a thousand years. Other Celtic tribes who seem to have arrived later include: the Érainn, who are thought to have colonized the south of the country and from whom the name Ireland is ultimately derived; the Laighin who conquered the east of the country, in the areas now covered by counties Kilkenny, Wexford and Carlow; and finally the Gaeil, who arrived from Roman Gaul around 50 BC and ultimately conquered the earlier arrivals. It is important to realize, however, that although the Gaelic culture and society dominated the country for the next 16 centuries, it did so by absorbing rather than eliminating its predecessors. Traces of the earlier Celts and, no doubt, of the Neolithic culture are present in Gaelic society.

Gaelic Society

The largest division in the Gaelic society was between the tribes of the south, the Eoghanacht, taking their collective name from their ancestor/god Eogan, and the Connachta, based in the west and north and named after Conn, brother of Eogan. The Eoghanacht dynasty founded at Cashel *c.* AD 400 dominated Munster up to the twelfth century. The Munster families O'Sullivan, McCarthy and O'Connell were all formed of Eoghanacht stock. Of the Connachta, by far the most important tribe were the Uí Néill, who descended from Niall Noigiallach, Niall of the Nine Hostages, given in the Gaelic pseudo-genealogies as a direct descendant of Conn. The Uí Néill conquered the north-west and east of the country in the fifth and sixth centuries and established separate dynasties with seats of power at Inishowen in Donegal and Tara in Meath. Separate Connachta tribes, the Uí Ailella, Uí Fiachrach, and Uí Briain held sway in Connacht itself. In addition other, less powerful groupings controlled south-western Ulster (the Oirialla) and eastern Ulster (the Ulaidh).

Within the larger divisions outlined above, a series of smaller petty kingdoms or *tuatha* existed, about 150 in all, each with its own over-lord owing allegiance to a more powerful regional or provincial leader. Underlying these political divisions, there was a remarkable cultural consistency throughout the island. In typical Celtic fashion, there were highly elaborate rules governing the interactions between families, classes, kin-groups and *tuatha*. The interpretation and application of these was regulated by a hereditary class of professional jurists, part of a larger professional class known as the *aos dána* which included poets, historians (in reality genealogists), musicians and druids. Patronage of these professionals was in the hands of the free (*saor aicme*) who had property and family rights. There were also many slaves. The feudal notion of primogeniture, inheritance through the eldest son, was completely alien to this society. Instead property rights inhered in a much more broadly defined family, the *fine*, all the male descendants of a common great-grandfather.

It is not surprising, given the proliferation of political divisions, the tribal loyalties and the complexity of the legal system, that conflict was a constant feature of Gaelic society. Up to the end of the Middle Ages there was unceasing warfare, between the Eoghanachta and the Uí Néill, between *tuatha*, between and within *fine*.

Christianity

Up to the sixteenth century, when the English conquest began in earnest, the single most profound outside influence on Gaelic culture was the coming of Christianity. The monastic ideas of the fifth-century missionaries were rapidly assimilated, the clerical hierarchy of the monks reflecting the kinds of hierarchies in secular society, with the result that by the end of the sixth century more than eight hundred monasteries had been founded, and their confederations became like powerful *tuatha* in their own right. Many offices of the Church became hereditary within the *fine*, like the kingships. The Irish term was *erenach*.

Although they were evidently skilled in the ways of temporal power, it was for their learning and missionary fervour that Irish monks became famous. Between AD 600 and 900 Irish monasteries were founded throughout continental Europe and Britain, and their scribes produced some of the masterpieces of early medieval illumination.

The Vikings

Remaining outside the borders of the Roman Empire, Ireland had not experienced an invasion since the arrival of the Gael. Then, at the end of the eighth century, the Viking attacks began; for more than two centuries these had a devastating effect on monastic culture in particular.

The Vikings were Danish, Norwegian or Swedish traders, fishermen and small farmers who were forced into a life of nomadic plunder on the seas by the pressures of over-population. At the outset their raids were infrequent and piecemeal but soon developed into large systematic attacks using fleets of longships which could navigate the rivers and lakes and penetrate deep inland. From the early ninth century, Viking settlements began to emerge around the sea-coast, the most important being Dublin, which survived as an independent Danish kingdom until the twelfth century.

The political power of the Vikings was broken at the Battle of Clontarf in 1014, and they were soon assimilated into Gaelic culture. Probably their most significant legacy was the creation of the first Irish towns. Gaelic culture was essentially rural, with the monasteries and their satellite settlements serving as trading centres. Wexford, Dublin, Cork, Waterford and Limerick were all originally Viking.

The Normans

The Normans were descendants of Viking settlers who has colonized the area in north-eastern France now known as Normandy and had become fiercely efficient in the conduct of warfare. In the eleventh century, they conquered England with only 5000 soldiers and established a strong feudal government, with an expanding presence in Scotland and Wales.

In 1169, as a result of the internecine wars of the Irish kings, the Normans were invited to Ireland and wasted no time in seizing their opportunity; by 1171, they were masters of most of the east of the country and over the next two centuries extended and consolidated their conquest. The process was not straightforward. As before, Gaelic culture absorbed the newcomers and many of the great Norman lords were soon acting, in effect, as Gaelic petty kings. The extent of the power of the kings of England over even their own followers in Ireland remained problematic until the sixteenth century.

The Tudor Plantations

The relative laxity of Anglo-Norman rule in Ireland changed radically with the accession Henry Vlll to the throne of England. He demanded, and received, formal submission from the most powerful Gaelic and Norman leaders in return for English titles and legal recognition of their authority, and extended the areas of the country controlled directly by the Crown. Under his daughter Mary, the process of Plantation began: land held by the existing lords was declared forfeit to the Crown, on a variety of pretexts, and granted to English settlers. The earliest attempts in counties Laois and Offaly (renamed Queen's and King's respectively) were failures, due to the fierce resistance of the existing inhabitants. Elizabeth continued the policy, most notably in Munster, where attempts were made to settle the confiscated lands of the Earl of Desmond. This too was severely disrupted by local resistance, but most especially by the great rebellion which began in 1594, when O'Neill, O'Donnell and Maguire, the Ulster lords whose rule had been least affected by the Normans or by the sixteenth-century encroachments of the Crown, in effect declared war on English rule in Ireland.

The Ulster Plantation

The effects of the defeat of the rebellion in 1601 were felt most acutely in Ulster. All of the Gaelic leadership was forced to flee abroad, and in 1609 all of counties Armagh, Cavan, Coleraine (now Derry), Fermanagh and Tyrone were forfeited to the Crown and the Plantation of Ulster began. In addition, privately-sponsored plantations took place in Antrim and Down, where centuries of contact across the North Channel had already created a strong Scottish presence. Unlike the earlier southern plantations, the Ulster Plantation was highly successful and attracted a massive influx of settlers, most of them Scottish dissenters attracted as much by the relative freedom of worship in a frontier territory as by the prospect of land.

The Seventeenth Century

Apart from the northern Plantation, the seventeenth century saw a general and massive transfer of land ownership from the Catholic Irish, precipitated by the final collapse of Gaelic power. Whereas at the start of the century 90% of the land area of the country was in the hands of the Catholic Irish, by the end of the century the figure was only 14%. The new owners were for the most part settlers, such as Cromwellian soldiers and officers, 'adventurers', 'New English' and non-Catholic, as opposed to the earlier Anglo-Normans, the 'Old English' who had in the main stayed Catholic.

One of the most important provisions of the Treaty of Limerick (1691) which marked King William's final defeat of the Jacobite Irish – the Gaelic aristocracy and their followers who had fought in the cause of the Catholic King James – was to allow the officers and men of the beaten army to go into exile. More than 11,000 men sailed to France in the Flight of the Wild Geese, and formed the famous Irish Brigade in the French army. This was the start of a long military connection between the remnants of the old Gaelic nobility and the armies of the Catholic kings of Europe; in the following century as many as 500,000 Irishmen joined the French army alone.

Huguenots and Palatines

As Irish conditions became more settled around the start of the eighteenth century, two groups of continental Protestant refugees made their way to Ireland with official, or semi-official help. The first of these, the Huguenots, were French Calvinists persecuted intermittently by the Catholic rulers of France throughout the seventeenth century. Small numbers of refugees from this persecution had come to Ireland, mainly via England, between 1620 and 1641, and again with Cromwell in 1649. But it was in 1685, after the revocation of the Edict of Nantes which had guaranteed them toleration, that the main body of Huguenots began to arrive, mostly from the countryside around the city of La Rochelle in the modern region of Poitou-Charente. After the end of the Williamite wars, large Huguenot settlements were established in Portarlington, Youghal, Cork, Dublin, Waterford and Lisburn, where they became celebrated for their expertise in textiles, specialising in weaving, lace-making, and glove-making. In the course of time, they became thoroughly absorbed into Irish society through intermarriage, and names such as Boucicault, Maturin, Le Fanu and Trench are still familiar in Ireland today.

The second wave of Protestant refugees were the Palatine Germans. In early May 1709, thousands of the inhabitants of the countryside of Hesse and Baden, near the city of Mannheim, were forced off their land by the wars between Louis XIV and a confederacy that included England. They made their way to Rotterdam and, from there, to London in English ships. The English appear to have been ill-prepared to receive them, and over 800 families, more than 6000 people, were dispatched to Ireland between September 1709 and January 1710.

Initially, there was some difficulty in placing the Palatines; of 538 families first taken on as tenants by Anglo-Irish landlords, 352 were reported to have deserted their holdings, and a good number of these returned to England. However, some of the settlements were highly successful, in particular that on the Southwell lands around Rathkeale in Co. Limerick in 1712. Some 150 families settled here on very favourable terms, and within a few years were fully engaged in the production of hemp, flax and cattle. A second successful, and sizable, settlement of Palatine families was carried out on the lands of Abel Ram, near Gorey in Co. Wexford around the same period. The distinctive Palatine way of life endured in these areas until well into the nineteenth century. Evidence of their eventual absorption into the life of the country is found today in the geographical spread of the distinctive surnames of their descendants – Switzer, Ruttle, Sparling, Tesky, Fitzell.

The Anglo-Irish

The eighteenth century saw the rise of a powerful, though ill-defined race, the Anglo-Irish. These were a social élite, dominating politics, the law, land, and the professions, who were descended from Norman, Old English, Cromwellian or even, in some rare cases, Old Gaelic stock. Rather than a common ethnic origin, what defined this people was membership of the state church, the Church of Ireland, and a strong if unlikely sense of belonging, derived from a confused colonial nationalism. This is reflected in their use of the word 'Irish'. Those who, in 1690, were 'the Protestants of Ireland' or 'the English of this Kingdom', by the 1720s could call themselves, simply, 'Irish gentlemen'; whereas previously, 'Irish' had meant 'native Irish', it was now extended to cover those who had been outsiders. There remained, however, a fatal ambiguity in its use. The continuing threat posed to the position of the Anglo-Irish by the overwhelming majority of the population – Gaelic, Catholic, and living in a degree of poverty that astounded foreign observers – meant that they simply could not afford to identify too closely with the country as a whole. As a result, in the writings of the time, 'the Irish', or even 'the Irish race' most often refers specifically to the people we now call Anglo-Irish.

Although real power emanated from London, within Ireland the Anglo-Irish were dominant for over two centuries, and much of the character of the country today derives from their influence. They were responsible for the great neo-classical houses of the gentry, the Georgian buildings and thoroughfares of Dublin, and the literary tradition which lay behind the great revival of writing in Ireland in the early twentieth century.

Ulster Emigration

For the Scottish dissenters and their descendants who had come to Ireland hoping for religious and economic freedom, the rise of the Anglo-Irish and the legal framework created to enshrine their ascendancy represented fresh enslavement. In addition, the increasing commercial pressures brought to bear by landlords and a series of natural disasters through the eighteenth century meant growing hardship for many. One result was the radicalisation of dissenting political opinion, which saw its culmination in the Presbyterian participation in the rebellion of 1798; another was the slow growth over the century of emigration from Ulster to America. By 1790 the United States population of Irish stock had reached almost half-a-million, the vast majority of them of Ulster extraction.

The Scots-Irish, as they called themselves in North America, brought their radical opinions with them and were disproportionately represented in the American War of Independence and in the subsequent political life of the United States.

Nineteenth-Century Emigration

Until the early nineteenth century, emigration was not a realistic option for the vast majority of the Catholic Irish; tradition, law, poverty and lack of opportunity created virtually insurmountable barriers and only a trickle of newcomers reached the New World. After the end of the Napoleonic Wars in 1814 and the repeal of restrictions on Catholic emigration in 1828, however, emigration did begin and the numbers rose steadily throughout the 1830s and 1840s, spurred on by the succession of harsh winters, crop failures and epidemics experienced sporadically throughout the country. By the mid 1840s, the eve of the Great Famine, large numbers were already leaving. It was the catastrophe of the Famine, however, that opened the floodgates. Faced with the prospect of destitution and death – over a million died between 1845 and 1848 – desperation gripped the population and more than a million and a half left the country in less than five years. The demoralising effect of the disaster on the country was such that even after famine had receded, the numbers leaving continued to be enormous. Uniquely among European countries, an Irish population of almost eight million recorded in the census of 1841 had shrunk to just over four million by 1921.

By the 1920s, emigration on the nineteenth-century scale had ceased. There was still a significant flow of migrants up to the 1960s, mainly to Britain, and still the same sense of defeat that the country could not support its own people. Only since the late 1980s has the flow stopped completely, and even reversed. The growth of prosperity and national self-confidence achieved over two or three decades has been remarkable and, one hopes, irreversible.

Origins and Evolution of Surnames in Ireland

Personal names

Naming is the most fundamental function of language, the verbal equivalent of pointing. On the most mundane level personal names, the combinations of first name and family name (or surname) which distinguish us from each other, are merely identifying tags. But providing a label is the least important business of names. Personal names do of course designate and distinguish individuals, but they also embody a nexus of links with family, society, culture and history whose simplest lesson is that we belong somewhere.

Personal names have existed as long as there has been language. In earliest times, individuals were given single words which tended to be simple or metaphorical descriptives (the Celtic Artos, meaning 'bear', for example) or compounds very often religious in origin, such as Devadatta (Sanskrit) and Theodoros (Greek), both meaning 'given by God', Hannibal (Carthaginian), meaning 'grace of Baal' (a god), Abdullah (Arabic), or 'slave of Allah'. More secular compounds were also common. Examples include the Celtic Vercingetorix ('great king of warriors'), the Slavic Miroslav, bringing together the words for 'world' and 'glory', and the Germanic Frideriko, combining 'peace' and 'powerful'.

In the course of time, as the stock of names became standardised and populations increased, a second name became necessary to distinguish individuals bearing the same personal name – so you had John Brown-hair, John Bill's-son, John the Thatcher and John from-Ballymore. These were not surnames as we think of them, passed through the generations, but still individual identifiers. They fell into the four broad categories of the examples given, respectively descriptive, patronymic, occupational and toponymic. Some notable exceptions to these categories do exist of course. The American Indians used surnames related to totemic animals or auspicious events, such as Little Deer or Wounded Bear.

Of the four major categories outlined, by far the largest is the patronymic, indicating the individual's parentage. There are obvious reasons for this. In most cultures the most important component of individual identity was and still is the network of family relationships, for which parentage is the clearest shorthand. In Ireland, all of the native Irish surnames which emerged, without exception, were patronymic − a clear indication of the significance of kinship in Gaelic society.

The origins of hereditary surnames

The Chinese were the earliest to introduce hereditary surnames; the practice of continuing surnames from father to children was widespread as early as the fourth century BC, with the Confucian respect for ancestors no doubt playing a role. In Europe, the Romans had an elaborate naming system throughout the Republican and the Imperial periods. Initially, there were only two elements, the *preanomen*, equivalent to the modern first name, and the *nomen*, the name of the *gens* or clan-group. Since both were severely restricted, eventually another element was added, the *cognomen*, which belonged to the specific family within the clan-group and which was truly hereditary. This system, producing such familiar names as Gaius Julius Caesar for example, remained stable until the Empire began to decline. But after the third century AD, as the number of freed slaves grew and Roman citizenship expanded dramatically, so many people were adopting names which had no connection with family or *gens* that the names began to lose their significance.

It was not until the tenth and eleventh centuries that true

hereditary surnames or family names began to emerge once again in Europe. Why this should have been can only be guessed at. The practice appears to have begun with wealthy and noble families and gradually spread to other classes and it may have been that securing inheritance rights played a part. The beginnings of the centralised European states, with their record-keeping needs and the necessity for stable identifers may also have been a factor. Or it might simply have been the pressure of population growth.

Whatever the reasons, hereditary family surnames began to appear throughout Europe from the tenth century and the process was largely complete by the start of the seventeenth century.

Evolution of surnames in Ireland

In Ireland as elsewhere in Europe, surnames were not hereditary up until the tenth century. While many of the names appearing in accounts of this time appear similar in form to modern Irish names, incorporating in particular the prefix 'Mac' (meaning 'son of'), in fact they were not hereditary, lasting only one generation. Thus Conor mac Airt, was Conor, son of Art; his own son would be Turlough mac Conor, son of Conor.

Nonetheless, Ireland was one of the first European countries in which a system of fixed hereditary surnames developed. The earliest names appear to be those incorporating 'O' or its earlier form 'Ua', meaning 'grandson'. The first recorded fixed surname seems to be O'Clery (Ó Cléirigh), as noted by the *Annals*, which record the death of Tigherneach Ua Cléirigh, lord of Aidhne in Co. Galway in the year 916. One of the earliest authorities on Irish names claims this as the oldest hereditary surname recorded anywhere in Europe.

When the process of creating family names got fully underway, it reflected the importance of the Church in medieval Irish life. Many common modern Irish surnames dating from this period include 'Gil-' or 'Kil-', an anglicised version of the Irish *Giolla*, meaning follower or devotee. Thus Gilmartin, in Irish Mac Giolla Mhairtin, means 'son of a follower of (St) Martin'. Similarly, the Church is the origin of all of those names starting with 'Mul-', a version of the Irish *Maol*, meaning bald, and applied to the monks because of their distinctive tonsure. Thus Mulrennan (O Maoilbhreanainn) means 'descendant of a follower of St. Brendan'.

By the eleventh century, many families had acquired true hereditary surnames as we would know them today. All of these incorporate the same two basic elements, 'O' or 'Mac', together with the personal name of the ancestor from whom descent is indicated. In many cases this ancestor can be quite accurately identified and the origin of the name dated precisely. Thus, at the start of the eleventh century, Brian Ború possessed no surname, being simply Brian, High-King of the Irish. His grandson Teigue called himself Ua Briain in memory of his illustrious grandfather, and the name became hereditary thereafter. Similarly, the O'Neills derive their surname from Niall mac Aoidh, who died in 917.

Due to linguistic changes, the origins of many of the personal names such as Niall or Brian which form the stem of the surname remain obscure, but two broad categories can be distinguished: descriptive and occupational. In the first category, we can guess that the progenitor of the Traceys (Ó Treasaigh) was a fierce character, *treasach* meaning 'war-like', while the ancestor of the Duffys must have been dark-featured, since *dubh*, the root of the name, means black or dark. Among the occupations recorded in names are the churchmen dealt with above, spokesman (MacCloran, Mac Labhráin, from the Irish *labhraidh*), bard (Ward, Mac an Bhaird, from bard), clerks or clerics (Clery, Ó Cléirigh, from *cléireach*), and smiths (McGowan, Mac Gabhainn, from *gabhann*). One category of name, common in English, which is extremely rare among Irish names is the toponymic, deriving from the name of a locality. Yourell, from the kingdom of Oriel in the north has been claimed as the only Gaelic toponymic. For the Gaeil, evidently, who you were related to was much more important than where you came from.

Although it began early, the process of the creation of surnames was slow, and continued for over six hundred years. As the population grew and new families were formed, they sought to consolidate their identity by adopting hereditary surnames of their own, usually by simply adding 'Mac' to the first name of the founding ancestor. In the course of this process, then, many surnames were created which are, in fact, offshoots of more common names. Thus, for example, the MacMahons and the McConsidines of Clare are descended from the O'Brien family, the former from Mahon O'Brien, who died in 1129, the latter from Constantine O'Brien, who died in 1193, while the MacMahons of Fermanagh are descended from Mahon Maguire, a grandson of Donn Carrach Maguire. The continuing division and sub-division of the most powerful Gaelic families like this is almost certainly the reason for the great proliferation of Gaelic surnames.

Non-Gaelic sources of surnames

Viking

From the start of the ninth century, more than a hundred years before the adoption of hereditary surnames began, the Vikings were a constant presence and a constant threat throughout Ireland, consolidating and extending their power through unremitting aggression. When their political power declined after 1014, as a people the Vikings were soon thoroughly absorbed into the religious and political life of the country, adopting the Irish language and Irish customs, intermarrying and intermingling. Since the practice of hereditary surnames had not become widespread, no Irish surnames are actually Danish or Norwegian in origin, but many modern Irish surnames reflect Viking origins, grafting the Gaelic prefixes to personal names introduced by the Vikings. Examples include McLoughlin (Mac Lochlainn) McAulliff (Mac Amlaoimh – more familiar as 'Olaf') and McIvor (Mac Iomhair).

Norman

The extent of the intermingling of Norman and Gaelic is illustrated graphically in the history of surnames of Norman origin. These are numerous and widespread throughout the country, and most of them were created in the aftermath of the Norman invasion, names such as Browne, Burke, Cusack, Keating, Power, Walsh. Whatever their current form, virtually all of these originated in Norman-French, either linked to a particular placename in Normandy or Wales, or as a French descriptive. Thus de Burgo or de Burgh, the original version of Burke, comes from Tonburg in Normandy, while le Poer, the original for Power, comes from *le povre*, meaning 'the poor one'. The names now most obviously as of Norman origin are those beginning with 'Fitz', a corruption of the French *fils*, meaning 'son', and used by the Normans in the same way as the Gaels used 'Mac'. Of course, as well as those of purely Norman origin, the twelfth-century invaders also included many of Breton and Flemish extraction. Irish names of Breton origin include Dillon (de Leon, from Leon in Brittany) and Brett (le Breton), while Flemish examples include Fleming, Roche (de la Roche), Barry (de Barri) and Wall (de Vale).

As the Normans were assimilated into Gaelic culture, their surnames underwent the same process of subdivision already seen in Gaelic surnames. Thus, for example, in the thirteenth century the descendants of Piers de Birmingham were calling themselves MacFheorais, Irish for 'son of Piers', which was later anglicised as Corish. In the same way, Jocelyn (in Irish Goisdelbh) de Angulo was the ancestor of the family of Mac Goisdealbhaigh, anglicised Costello, while the fragmentation of the powerful de Burgo (Burke) family of Connacht led to such surname offshoots as MacWalter, MacSeonin (later anglicised as Jennings), MacMyler and MacDavid.

Settler

The old Gaelic world never recovered from its final collapse in the seventeenth century. Although vestiges of the old culture survived underground in poetry, music and folklore, English ways were now dominant, and this extended even to the old surnames. From about this time, the prefixes 'O' and 'Mac' began to be dropped, and the names themselves were anglicised and distorted. English officials and landlords, unfamiliar with Irish, transliterated, translated, and mistranslated. Thus, for example, Ó hArrachtáin, common in Cork and Kerry, was changed to Harrington, its nearest-sounding English equivalent. Some changes are mystifying; how even the most cloth-eared English administrator could have thought Ó Brolcháin, common in Donegal, was the equivalent of the English 'Bradley' remains an enigma, but Bradleys they now are. Other names were translated: Mac Gabhain (son of the smith) becoming Smith in some areas, while remaining McGowan in others, and Mac Giolla Easpaig (son of the follower of the bishop) becoming either Gillespie or, simply, Bishop. A large number of ludicrous mistranslations also date from this time. To take one example only, Mac an Dheaghanaigh (son of the dean) became Bird in many places, because of a spurious phonetic resemblance to the Irish for bird, *éan*. Previous Gaelic attitudes to such names underline the sharp ironies of this process. When the influx of settlers began in the seventeenth century, the Gaelic poets ridiculed the new surnames; in Irish society, the function of the surname, with 'O' or 'Mac', was to indicate kinship, and such names as White, Black, Bird or Smith were ridiculously absurd. Within less than a century, the names they had mocked were being forced on them.

The History of Heraldry in Ireland

Heraldry is the study and description of coats of arms, and of the rights of individuals and families to bear arms. It began in the first half of the twelfth century, as a result of developments in medieval weaponry and armour in continental Europe. The old coats of chain-and-link mail, with long shields, gave way to full-body plate armour and helmets encasing the entire head, with smaller triangular shields. Individual knights thus became completely anonymous. The necessity for markings on their shields to identify themselves in battles and in tournaments is self-evident.

At first, this military necessity was the determining factor. Large, clearly identifiable patterns, involving two or three colours divided into a number of compartments related to the physical construction of the shield make up the earliest arms. Later, when animals and other symbols were added, the necessity for easy, quick recognition again meant that a large degree of stylised convention was used, so that the heraldic lion, for instance, bears only a slight resemblance to the real thing.

The military origin of arms is also the most likely explanation for their emergence at almost exactly the same time in England, France, Germany and Italy. The eight Christian crusades against Islam between 1096 and 1271 involved knights from all of these countries, and, combined with the changes in armour, provided a context in which a system of military recognition was essential. The endurance of heraldry is no doubt partly due to the fact that it spread over the whole of Europe virtually simultaneously. Crosses and fleurs-de-lis, Christian symbols *par excellence*, also take their origins in heraldry from the Crusades.

But heraldry would long ago have died out completely if the only need it met was military. Individual recognition and family identity are both powerful and universal human needs and, towards the end of the thirteenth century, a further change came about as the social and non-military aspects of heraldry evolved and it became established that coats of arms were personal and hereditary. The symbols used could now relate to the name, the office or the territory of the bearer, and were dictated less by the imperative of immediate recognition. One of the results was the creation of so-called 'canting' arms, based on a pun on the name – in Ireland, the arms of the Aherne family, displaying three herons, are an example. The main non-military use of arms was on seals, as a means of proving the authenticity of documents, and the practice of using birds or animals to fill empty space around the arms on these seals gave rise to 'supporters', now regarded as part of the arms of peers. Eventually, arms were also used on tombs, and then on works of art and possessions.

The symbols used in heraldry have a variety of origins: in the Christian nature of the crusades, in the (supposed) character of the individual or family itself, in some event which is identified with the family. There is no strict attachment of significance to particular symbols, although the reasons for some symbols are self-evident; the lion is conventionally regal, the unicorn is a symbol of purity, the boar is a Celtic symbol of endurance and courage, and so on.

As arms proliferated, a natural need arose for rules to prevent different individuals and families using the same or similar symbols and arrangements of symbols. The first result was the evolution of the peculiar technical vocabulary used in describing arms, a highly stylised and extremely precise mixture of early French, Latin and English, still used in heraldry today. Then came the creation of the offices of King of Arms or King of Heralds throughout most of

Europe in the fourteenth century. The principal functions of these were the recognition of arms, the recording of their possession, the granting of arms and adjudication in disputes between bearers of arms. By the end of the fifteenth century, since the right to bear arms depended on family and ancestry, they had also become genealogists.

Irish Heraldic Traditions

Arms first arrived in Ireland with the Normans, who brought with them all the social structures on which European heraldry depended; until that time, although some evidence of the use of military symbolism among the Gaels survives, heraldry in the true sense did not exist. Norman heraldry shows clearly its military origins, with a preponderance of clear, simple devices (known as 'ordinaries') designed for easy recognition, such as those found in the arms of the de Burgos, de Clares, Fitzgeralds and others of Norman extraction.

A separate heraldic tradition is found in the arms of the Anglo-Irish. This can be dated to the mid-sixteenth century, when the Tudor monarchs of England began to address themselves seriously to taking possession of Ireland, and establishing the full panoply of English law. Accordingly, the Office of Ulster King of Arms, with authority over all arms in Ireland, was set up in 1552, as part of the household of the Vice-Regal Court, the administration of the English King's deputy in Ireland. Inevitably, the early records of the Office contain many examples of Anglo-Irish heraldic practice, characterised by great elaboration, with individual shields often containing as many as a dozen charges, reflecting the preoccupations of the Anglo-Irish with family relationships. Whereas Norman arms are clearly military, the arms of the Anglo-Irish are part of a much more settled society, concerned, above all, about status.

The third tradition of heraldry in Ireland relates to the original inhabitants, the Gaelic Irish, and is more problematic, since heraldry was a natural aspect of the social life of both Normans and Anglo-Irish, but originally had no part in Gaelic society. The characteristics of the arms in use among the important Gaelic families do have a number of common features, however. In part this is due to the role of genealogy in early Irish society. The myth of a common origin was a potent means of unifying the different Celtic and pre-Celtic peoples of Ireland, and the enormously elaborate Gaelic pseudo-genealogies, tracing every family in the country back to the same individual, were designed to reinforce that myth. In addition, on a more mundane level, the nature of Gaelic law meant that, in effect, what you could own depended on who you were related to. These two factors, the importance of the origin myth and the property rights of the extended family, are reflected in the heraldic tradition which grew up in Ireland from about the fifteenth century.

Unlike the military simplicity of the Normans or the conventional elaborations of the Anglo-Irish, the symbols used in the arms of Gaelic Irish families tend to relate to pre-Christian myths, often in quite obscure ways. Thus, for example, the Red Hand of the O'Neills, now also associated with the province of Ulster, in heraldic terms *a dexter hand appaumé gules*, also occurs in various forms in the arms of other Gaelic families. The reason would appear to lie in the name of the son of Bolg or Nuadu, the Celtic sun-god, in some accounts the divine ancestor of all the Celts. This son was known as Labraid Lamhdearg, or Labraid of the Red Hand. The association with the ancestral power of the sun-god is clearly a very good reason for the choice of symbol.

In a similar way, the stag which appears in the arms of many Munster families – MacCarthy, O'Sullivan, Healy and many others – relates very clearly to the kingship myth of the Erainn peoples. In this myth, the legitimacy of the ruling house is confirmed when a stag enters; the animal is hunted, and the border of the territory is defined by the chase; the future ruler is the individual who eventually slays the stag. The many families displaying the stag in their arms were originally part of the great Eoghanacht tribal grouping which dominated Munster until the time of Brian Ború. The stag was self-evidently an appropriate choice of symbol.

As in Ulster and Munster, so in Connacht: the arms of the ruling family, the O'Conors, and of a whole host of others connected with them – Flanagan, O'Beirne and many others – all display a common symbol, in this case the oak tree. Again, the reason lies in pre-Christian Celtic reverence for the oak, and its association with kingship; the medieval sources record ruling families having at least one sacred tree outside the family's ring-fort.

As well as the association of heraldic symbolism with pre-Christian myth, the nature of the property relations within the extended family meant that arms were used in ways quite different to those practiced among the Normans and Anglo-Irish. In particular, most of the arms were regarded as the property of the sept (defined by Dr Edward MacLysaght as 'a group of persons inhabiting the same locality and bearing the same surname'), rather than being strictly hereditary within a single family, as was and is the case under English and Scottish heraldic law.

In summary, two of the three heraldic traditions in Ireland – the Norman and the Anglo-Irish – form part of the mainstream of European heraldry, while the arms found among the Gaelic Irish have particular characteristics which set them apart.

Irish Heraldic Authority

The Genealogical Office is the successor to the Office of Ulster

King of Arms which, as noted above, was created in 1552 with full jurisdiction over arms in Ireland. Ulster retained this power for almost four centuries until 1943, when the title was transferred to the College of Arms in London and the office of Chief Herald of Ireland was created to continue to fulfill the functions of Ulster in independent Ireland. The new name given to the Office of the Chief Herald, 'The Genealogical Office', was inaccurate, since its primary concern continues to be heraldic rather than genealogical.

Over the first 150 years of its existence, the Office was almost exclusively concerned with Anglo-Irish heraldry, recording, registering and legitimising the practice of arms that had grown up. From the start of the eighteenth century, Ulster began to acquire other duties as an officer of the Crown intimately linked to the government. These duties were largely ceremonial, deciding and arranging precedence on state occasions, as well as introducing new peers to the Irish House of Lords and recording peerage successions. When the chivalric Order of St. Patrick was introduced in 1783 as an Irish equivalent of such long-established English institutions as the Order of the Garter, Ulster became its registrar, responsible for administering its affairs. He also continued to have responsibility for the ceremonial aspects of state occasions at the court of the English Viceroy. The heraldic and ceremonial duties of Ulster continued down to the twentieth century.

Today the Office of the Chief Herald remains principally concerned with the granting of arms to individuals and corporate bodies, the ceremonial aspect having lapsed with the establishment of the Republic of Ireland. One aspect of the Office's work today is perhaps connected to this, however. This is the practice of recognising Chiefs of the Name, instituted in the 1940s by Dr Edward MacLysaght, the first Chief Herald. The aim was simply to acknowledge the descendants of the leading Gaelic Irish families, and this was done by uncovering the senior descendants in the male line of the last Chief of the Name duly inaugurated as such under the old Gaelic laws. The practice is a courtesy only; under Irish law no native hereditary titles are recognised.

Irish
Family
Names

Aherne

HERALDIC BLAZON
Vert, three herons Argent

Aherne is an anglicisation of Ó Echtigerna, from Echtigern meaning 'lord of horses', and is also found in the variants Hearn and Hearne. An earlier and phonetically closer version was O'Hagerin. Echtigern was a relatively common personal name in Gaelic society, borne by a nephew of Brian Ború, for instance. The surname originated, in fact, in the sept or tribe of Brian, the Dál gCais, and has always been strongly associated with their homeland in Co. Clare. The family territory was in the south-east of the county, around Sixmilebridge. At an early date, however, the entire family and their descendants appear to have been forced to migrate from this ancestral territory; one source records them being driven out by the MacNamaras in the early fourteenth century. At any rate, by the mid-seventeenth century the surname is not recorded as one of the principal Irish names of Co. Clare, appearing instead in east Cork and Waterford. In Cork the family were followers of the Hiberno-Norman lords of the area, the Fitzgerald earls of Desmond, and Lord Roche.

In 1890 122 births of the forms Ahern/Aherne were recorded, principally in counties Cork and Limerick, while 15 of the form Hearne/Herne/Hearn were noted, mainly in Co. Waterford. To this day, the name remains most numerous in these three counties.

The arms of the family include three herons, in an obvious pun on the name.

Famous Names

JOHN AHERON (c.1720-c.1780)

The first Irish architect who designed and built for Irish conditions. His *General Treatise on Architecture* (Dublin, 1754) is regarded as the foundation of Irish architecture.

JAMES A. HEARNE (1840-1901)

Born in New York, this son of Irish Aherne immigrants had tremendous success with his two plays *Hearts of Oak* and *Share Acres*.

PATRICIO LAFCADIO HEARNE (1850-1904)

Born in Greece, the son of a Co. Westmeath surgeon and a Greek mother, Lafcadio Hearn is remembered for his writings on Japan, where he lived   and worked for the last years of his life. In that country he has remained something of a national hero.

BERTIE AHERN (b. 1952)

The leader of Fianna Fáil, the largest political party in the Republic of Ireland. He has been Minister of Labour and Minister of Finance in previous governments.

Barrett

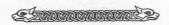

HERALDIC BLAZON
Barry of ten per pale argent
and gules countercharged

The name Barrett is now concentrated in two widely separated parts of Ireland: Co. Cork and the Mayo–Galway area. The Irish version of the name is Baróid in the south and Baréid in the west, and this may reflect two separate origins. At any rate, families of the name first appeared in these areas in the thirteenth century, after the Anglo-Norman invasion. Its Norman origin derives from the old Germanic personal name, Bernard or Beraud. A separate derivation gives its origin as the Middle English 'Barat', a nickname for a quarrelsome or deceitful person.

According to a pedigree of the Walshes of Mayo compiled in 1588 'Walynus', who arrived in Ireland in 1169, is said to have been the progenitor of the Walshes of Tirawley in Co. Mayo, and the brother of Barrett, the ancestor of the Barretts of Mayo. The western family, originally based around Killala, were thoroughly absorbed into Gaelic society very quickly. Their chief was known as Mac Bhaitin (or MacVattin) from Battin Barrett, who lived in the 13th century. This name may also have been anglicised as Padden, a name commonly found in Mayo today. In the middle ages the family began to split into various sub-clans, along Gaelic lines, and created a number of new surnames, among them McAndrew, Timmons and Roberts. The Cork settlers were not so Gaelicised, giving their name to the large barony of Barretts in the middle of the county.

The arms of the family are based on word play, a pictorial version of *barrettes*, in French 'short bars'.

TRADITIONAL FAMILY AREAS
Cork, Galway, Mayo

FAMILY RANKING
1890: 138th   *1996*: 132nd

NO. OF BIRTHS
1890: 146

Famous Names

RICHARD BARRETT (1740–1818)

This member of the Mayo family was well known as the 'Poet of Erris'
and was active in the United Irishmen.

MICHAEL BARRETT (d. 1868)

A member of the Fenians, Michael Barrett was the last man to suffer
a public hanging in England for his attempt to blow up
Clerkenwell prison.

PAUL BARRETT (b. 1954)

A well-known Dublin jazz musician and a trombonist of some note.

ROGER 'SYD' BARRETT (b. 1946)

A songwriter and guitarist who joined the rock group Pink Floyd
in 1966 and was instrumental in their rise to fame. Songs such as
Arnold Layne and *See Emily Play* (both 1967) were remarkable for their
unusual chord changes and psychedelic subject matter.

Barry

HERALDIC BLAZON
Argent three bars
gemels gules

The first bearer of the surname Barry to arrive in Ireland was Robert de Barri, one of the original band of Norman knights who landed at Bannow in Co. Wexford in May 1169, and a brother of Giraldus Cambrensis, the notoriously anti-Irish historian of the invasion. The name comes from the earlier association of the family with the island of Barry, seven miles south-west of Cardiff in Wales. From the start the family were prominent in the settlement of east Cork, and were soon absorbed into the native culture, forming subsepts on Gaelic lines, the most important being Barry Mor, Barry Óg and Barry Roe. The names of two of these are perpetuated in the names of the Cork baronies of Barrymore and Barryroe, and many other Cork placenames are linked to the family: Kilbarry, Rathbarry and Buttevant (from the family motto 'Boutez en avant'), to mention only three. The surname is now very numerous in Ireland, but still inextricably associated with Co. Cork.

As well as the Norman origin, two relatively uncommon Gaelic surnames Ó Beargha and Ó Baire have also been anglicised as Barry.

DEMOGRAPHIC DATA

TRADITIONAL FAMILY AREAS
Cork, Limerick, Waterford

FAMILY RANKING
1890: 72nd *1996*: 74th

NO. OF BIRTHS
1890: 217

Famous Names

JAMES BARRY (1741–1806)

A native of Cork city who was famed for his elaborate allegorical paintings and his portraits. He was a protégé of the philosopher Edmund Burke, and became professor of painting at the Royal Academy in 1782.

JOHN BARRY (1745–1803)

Wexford-born sailor who is known as 'Father of the American Navy' for his efforts at modernising the fleet during and after the War of American Independence.

KEVIN BARRY (1902–1920)

A medical student in Dublin when the War of Independence began, he became a member of the IRA. His capture and execution at the age of 18 made him a hero, and he is the subject of a famous eponymous ballad.

PETER BARRY (b. 1928)

Former deputy leader of the Fine Gael party (1979–1987) and Minister of Foreign Affairs (1982–1987). His family firm, Barry's of Cork, is Ireland's largest and oldest tea company.

SIR REDMOND BARRY (1813–1880)

An Irish-born Australian judge who became the first chancellor of the University of Melbourne and founded the National Gallery of Victoria.

Boyle

HERALDIC BLAZON
Or an oaktree
eradicated vert

Boyle, with its variants Boal and O'Boyle, is now one of the fifty most common surnames in Ireland; it was ranked 49th in 1890 and 46th in 1996. In Irish the name is Ó Baoghill, the derivation of which is uncertain, but thought to be connected to the old Irish *geall*, meaning 'pledge'. In the Middle Ages the family were powerful and respected, sharing control of the entire north-west of the island with the O'Donnells and the O'Dohertys, and the strongest association of the family is still with Co. Donegal, where (O')Boyle is the third most numerous name in the county.

The majority of those bearing the name are of Gaelic origin, but many Irish Boyles have separate, Norman origins. In Antrim and Down, a significant number are descended from the Scottish Norman family of de Boyville, whose name comes from the town now known as Beauville in Normandy; many Boals are thought to be of this connection. A Welsh branch of the same Norman family were the antecedents of the most famous Irish family of the surname, the Boyles, Earls of Cork and Shannon, descended from Richard Boyle, who arrived in Ireland from Kent in 1588 and quickly amassed enormous wealth. His earliest known ancestor was Humphrey de Binville, a Norman lord in Herefordshire in the eleventh century.

In 1890 there were 17 births giving the surname as Boal, principally in counties Antrim and Down; 20 O'Boyles mainly in Antrim and Mayo and 273 Boyles, in Antrim, Donegal and Mayo. In Co. Down the surname has also been anglicised as Bohill.

Famous Names

ROBERT BOYLE (1627–1691)

The son of the 1st Earl of Cork, he is best known – at least to generations of science students – as the formulator of Boyle's Law (stating that 'the volume of a fixed quantity of gas at a constant temperature is inversely proportional to its pressure'). His advocacy of scientific experimentation was extremely influential, and he was one of the founders of the Royal Society.

RICHARD BOYLE (1695–1753)

The 3rd Earl of Burlington and a great-grandson of the Earl of Cork. He is remembered today for his passion for Palladian architecture, in particular Burlington House in London.

JOHN J. BOYLE (1851–1922)

An American sculptor of Irish extraction, famous for his *Indian Family* in Lincoln Park in Chicago.

Brady

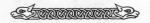

HERALDIC BLAZON

Sable, in the sinister base a dexter hand couped at the wrist proper pointing with index finger to the sun in splendour in dexter chief or

The surname derives from the Irish Mac Brádaigh, coming, possibly, from *brádach*, meaning 'thieving' or 'dishonest'. The name is among the sixty most frequently found in Ireland, and remains very numerous in Co. Cavan, their original homeland, with large numbers also to be found in the adjoining county of Monaghan. Their power was centred on an area a few miles east of Cavan town, from where they held jurisdiction over a large territory within the old Gaelic kingdom of Breifne. There have been many notable poets and clergymen of the name, including the satirical Gaelic poet Rev. Philip MacBrady and Fiachra MacBrady the Bard of Stradone as well as three MacBrady Bishops of Kilmore, and one MacBrady Bishop of Ardagh. The pre-Reformation Cavan Crozier, originally belonging to one of these MacBradys, is now to be found in the National Museum in Dublin.

A separate family, the Ó Gradáigh, of east Clare, have also anglicised their name as Brady.

Unlike many other Gaelic families, the 'Mac' prefix has not been reclaimed at all.

DEMOGRAPHIC DATA

TRADITIONAL FAMILY AREAS
Cavan, Longford, Monaghan

FAMILY RANKING
1890: 54th   *1996*: 51st

NO. OF BIRTHS
1890: 261

Famous Names

THOMAS BRADY (1752–1857)

Unlike many other Irishmen who served in European armies, Thomas Brady of Cootehill, Co. Cavan, came from farming stock. He became a Field Marshall in the Imperial Austrian army and governor of Dalmatia.

MATTHEW BRADY (c. 1823–1896)

A photographer noted for his photographs of the American Civil War. His collection, a part of which was purchased by the federal government in 1875, is unique in the annals of American photography, both for its magnitude and its realism.

PAUL BRADY (b. 1947)

Born in Strabane, Co. Tyrone, Paul Brady is one of Ireland's most successful contemporary musicians. His career has taken him from rock to traditional music and back again.

CONOR BRADY (b. 1949)

Eeditor of the *Irish Times* since 1985. A native of Tullamore, Co. Offaly, he has previously edited the *Sunday Tribune* and the *Garda Review*.

Brennan

Ó Branáin was a name found among the Cenel Eoghan, the tribal grouping claiming descent from Eoghan, one of the sons of the fourth-century monarch, Niall, progenitor of the Uí Néill. Their territory included the modern county which records his name, Tyrone, and it is in this area and the adjoining counties of Donegal, Fermanagh and Monaghan that the northern Brennans are now most commonly found. In this area, especially Donegal, the name was also anglicised as Brannan and Branny. It derives from three Irish originals: Ó Braonáin, from *braon*, possibly meaning 'sorrow', Mac Branáin, and Ó Branáin, both from *bran*, 'raven', one of the most popular early-Irish personal names.

Ó Braonáin originated in at least four distinct areas: Kilkenny, east Galway, Westmeath and Kerry. Of these the most powerful were the Ó Braonáin of Kilkenny, chiefs of Idough in the north of the county. After they lost their land and status to the English, many of them became notorious as leaders of bands of outlaws; witness the popular ballad *Brennan on the Moor*.

The Mac Branáin were chiefs of a large territory in the east of modern Co. Roscommon, and most Brennans of north Connacht, counties Mayo, Sligo and Roscommon, descend from them.

Found throughout the country, this is one of the commonest surnames in Ireland, though noticeably less so in Ulster. In 1890 it was ranked 27th, with 358 births, while in 1996 it was 14th in the Republic and only 91st in Northern Ireland. In 1890 15 Brannan births were also recorded, most of them in Donegal.

DEMOGRAPHIC DATA

TRADITIONAL FAMILY AREAS
Donegal, Fermanagh, Galway, Kerry,
Kilkenny, Monaghan, Roscommon,
Tyrone, West Meath

FAMILY RANKING
1890: 27th   *1996*: 22nd

NO. OF BIRTHS
1890: 358

Famous Names

JOHN BRENNAN (1768–1830)

One of the last chiefs of the name of the Kilkenny Brennans. He was popularly known as the 'wrestling doctor' for his satires on the Dublin medical establishment.

CHRISTOPHER (JOHN BRENNAN)

A classical scholar and the most learned poet Australia produced at the end of the 19th and the beginning of the 20th century. Mostly in the symbolist tradition, his work is characterized by force of feeling and depth of imagery.

JOSEPH BRENNAN (1887–1963)

One of the most influential Irish civil servants of his generation, he became the first Secretary of the Department of Finance, chairman of the Currency Commission and, from 1942 until 1953, first governor of the central Bank.

Burke

HERALDIC BLAZON
Or a cross gules, in the
dexter canton a lion
rampant sable

First of the name to arrive in Ireland was William Fitzadelm de Burgo, a Norman knight from Burgh in Suffolk, who took part in the 1171 invasion and succeeded Strongbow as Chief Governor. He received the earldom of Ulster and was granted vast tracts of territory in Connacht. His descendants adopted Gaelic customs and laws more completely than any other Norman invaders and were soon one of the most important families in the country. In Connacht, which remained the centre of the family's power, new septs formed on native Irish lines. William Liath de Burgh, a great-grandson of the original William, was the ancestor of the two most influential clans, the MacWilliam Uachtar of Co. Galway, and the MacWilliam Iochtar of Co. Mayo. Other descendants founded families which created distinct surnames: Philbin derives from Mac Philbin, son of Philip (de Burgh); Jennings, now common in Co. Galway, is an anglicisation of Mac Sheoinin, son of John (de Burgh); Gibbons, found in Mayo, was originally Mac Giobuin, son of Gilbert (de Burgh).

Burke, with its variants Bourke and de Burgh, is by far the most common Irish name of Norman origin, and its 20,000-plus Irish bearers probably represent only a fraction of the world-wide total.

According to legend, the arms of the family originated during the Crusades, when King Richard dipped his finger in the blood of a Saracen slain by one of the de Burghs, drew a cross on the Saracen's golden shield, and presented it to the victor. The motto 'Ung roy, Ung foy, Ung loy' translates as 'One king, one faith, one law', reflecting the loyalism of the most prominent branches of the family.

Famous Names

EDMUND BURKE (1729–97)

Dublin-born Edmund Burke was the most respected statesman of his time, a powerful opponent of political violence and political oppression.

WILLIAM BURKE (1792–1829)

With his partner William Hare, Corkman William Burke was the best-known of the nineteenth-century bodysnatchers. He procured fresh bodies for dissection in Edinburgh medical schools by the simple expedient of murder. 'To burke', meaning to smother, derives from his notoriety.

JOHN (1787–1848) AND SIR BERNARD BURKE (1814–92)

This father and son were altogether more respectable than their namesake above. Their works documenting the arms and pedigrees of the gentry and aristocracy, Burke's *Peerage and Baronetage*, Burke's *Landed Gentry*, Burke's *Irish Families*, Burke's *General Armory* (and many others) have been standard reference works for more than a century and a half. Sir Bernard became Ulster King of Arms, responsible for the regulation of arms in Ireland, precursor of the present Chief Herald of Ireland.

THOMAS BURKE (1740–83)

A descendant of Irish emigrants who held large estates in North Carolina, and was deeply involved in the War of American Independence. Burke County in North Carolina is named after him.

Butler

HERALDIC BLAZON
Quarterly: 1st and 4th, Or
a chief indented azure;
2nd and 3rd Gules three
covered cups or

The name Butler, found in England and Ireland, is Norman in origin and initially meant 'wine steward', from the same root as the modern French *bouteille*, 'bottle'. It came to denote the chief servant of a household and, in royal and powerful noble households, a high-ranking officer concerned only nominally with wine supply.

In Ireland the most prominent Butlers are descended from Theobald Fitzwalter, brother of the Archbishop of Canterbury, who was made 'Chief Butler' of Ireland by Henry II in 1177. The huge territories he was given were mainly in counties Tipperary, Wicklow and Limerick. His descendants were prolific and fertile: in the words of one of their own family historians, they bred 'like rabbits immune to myxomatosis'. There are now thought to be more than 9000 Butlers in Ireland.

They were also remarkably successful in collecting titles, acquiring no fewer than twenty-five separate patents of nobility, including such titles as Mountgarrett, Dunboyne, Ossory, Galmoy and Cahir. In 1328 they became the Earls of Ormond, their principal title, and James, the 12th earl, was created Duke of Ormond after the restoration of Charles II in 1660. From the Middle Ages to the twentieth century, their seat was Kilkenny Castle.

To the end of the seventeenth century, the Butlers were one of the most powerful Anglo-Norman dynasties, sharing effective control of Ireland with their great rivals the Fitzgeralds, earls of Desmond and earls of Kildare; the first Duke of Ormond was chancellor of Oxford and Dublin universities, Lord Lieutenant of Ireland, founder of the Royal College of Physicians and creator of Dublin's Phoenix Park.

TRADITIONAL FAMILY AREAS
Kilkenny, Limerick, Tipperary,
Wicklow

FAMILY RANKING
1890: 108th   *1996*: 101st

NO. OF BIRTHS
1890: 172

Famous Names

ELEANOR BUTLER (1745–1829)

The sister of the 17th Earl of Ormond who ran away with her neighbour,
Sarah Ponsonby, creating a huge scandal. The pair set up house together
in Wales where they became notorious as the Ladies of Llangollen.

EDWARD BUTLER (1823–79)

A Kilkenny native who edited the *Galway Vindicator* during the period of
the Young Ireland uprising, and subsequently emigrated to Australia,
where he became Attorney-General.

HUBERT BUTLER (1900–90)

Ireland's foremost political essayist, drawing sanity and intelligence from
his wide experience of Europe in the 1930s and '40s.

Byrne

HERALDIC BLAZON

Gules a chevron between three dexter hands couped at the wrist argent

Byrne or O'Byrne, together with its variants Beirne and Byrnes, is one of the ten most frequent surnames in Ireland today. In the original Irish the name is Ó Broin, from the personal name Bran, meaning 'raven'. It is traced back to Bran, son of Molmórda, a king of Leinster who ruled in the eleventh century.

As a result of the Norman invasion, the O'Byrnes were driven from their original homeland in Co. Kildare into south Co. Wicklow in the early thirteenth century. It was from Ballinacor in the valley of Glenmalure in that county that Fiach MacHugh O'Byrne waged his campaigns against the armies of Elizabeth I, with considerable success; his most noted victory was the defeat of Lord Grey in 1580. He was apprehended and executed in 1597. His son Phelim was the last chief of the O'Byrnes. He was finally dispossessed of his lands in 1628. The doings of the family in the sixteenth century are celebrated in the well-known *Leabhar Branach*, or Book of the O'Byrnes, a compilation of poetry in Irish put together in the late-seventeenth century. Even today, the vast majority of the Irish who bear the name originate in Wicklow or the surrounding counties. After the disasters of the seventeenth century some of these O'Byrnes migrated north to Ulster and changed their name to Burns, a Scottish surname common in east Ulster. In addition a separate Gaelic surname, Mac Broin, from the same root, *bran*, has been rendered Byrne, as well as the more usual McBrin.

Famous Names

CHARLES BYRNE (1768–88)

At almost eight-and-a-half feet tall, he became a freak show attraction known as the Irish Giant.

MYLES BYRNE (1780–1862)

A prominent participant in the 1798 rebellion who afterwards emigrated to France, where he had a distinguished career and was awarded the Legion d'Honneur. His *Memoirs* are renowned for their account of the rebellion.

ANDREW BYRNE (1802–62)

Andrew Byrne, born in Navan, Co. Meath, became a missionary to Native Americans and was ordained first Roman Catholic bishop of Little Rock.

GAY BYRNE (b. 1934)

Ireland's best-known and most influential broadcaster, 'Gaybo' has promoted discussion of topics hitherto considered taboo and has reflected and shaped social change for more than thirty years. His programme *The Late Late Show* has been among the highest-rated on Irish television since it began in 1962; it is now the world's longest-running television talk show.

Cahill

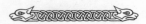

HERALDIC BLAZON
Argent a whale spouting in
the sea proper

The original Irish from which the name derives is Ó Cathail, from the common personal name Cathal, sometimes anglicised as Charles, which may in turn derive from the Old Irish *catu-ualos*, meaning 'strong in battle'.

Families of the name arose separately in different parts of Ireland, in Kerry, Galway, Tipperary and Clare. Originally the Galway family, located in the old diocese of Kilmacduagh near the Clare border, were most prominent, but their position was usurped by the O'Shaughnessys, and they declined. The southern families flourished, and the name is now most common in counties Cork, Kerry and Tipperary, while it is relatively infrequent in its other original homes. The arms illustrated are those of the Munster Cahills.

The geographical spread of families of the name is reflected in the forty-five placenames which incorporate Cahill. These placenames appear in Clare (four), Tipperary (six, including three Ballycahills), Galway (eight), Cork (two) and Kilkenny (one).

DEMOGRAPHIC DATA

TRADITIONAL FAMILY AREAS
Clare, Cork, Kerry, Tipperary

FAMILY RANKING
1890: 134th   *1996*: 142nd

NO. OF BIRTHS
1890: 147

Famous Names

FLANN O'CAHILL (d. 938)

A very early bearer of the name, whom the *Annals* record as having been martyred in 938.

FATHER DANIEL CAHILL (1796–1864)

Father Daniel Cahill was well known in his day as a teacher, journalist and lecturer.

Carroll

HERALDIC BLAZON
Sable two lions rampant
combatant or armed and
langued gules supporting a
sword point upwards proper
pommel and hilt of the first

One of the twenty-five commonest Irish surnames, Carroll (or O'Carroll) comes, in most cases from the Irish Ó Cearbhaill, 'grandson of Cearbhall', a very popular personal name thought to mean 'fierce in battle'. It is widespread today throughout Connacht, Leinster and Munster, reflecting the fact that it arose almost simultaneously as a separate surname in at least six different parts of Ireland. The most famous Ó Cearbhaill families were those based in Ely O'Carroll, an area covering modern Co. Offaly and parts of north Tipperary, and the O'Carroll, Princes of Oriel, a territory including most of the modern counties of Louth and Monaghan. Mac Cearbhaill, anglicised as MacCarroll and MacCarvill, was a separate surname based on the same root, and limited to Ulster.

The lords of Ely O'Carroll derived their name from Cearball, King of Ely, a leaders in the victorious native Irish army at Clontarf in 1014. Although their power was much reduced over the centuries in continuing conflict with the Norman Butlers, they kept their - distinctive Gaelic way of life until the start of the seventeenth century. The Oriel family lost most of their territory in the twelfth century as a result of the Norman invasion but remained powerful in church affairs.

The O'Carroll arms are those of the Oriel family, and may derive from a canting pun on the name of the race from whom the family claimed mythical descent, the Laighin, in Latin Gallinga, whence *dhá leon* (two lions). Lions are in any case a common heraldic symbol.

DEMOGRAPHIC DATA

TRADITIONAL FAMILY AREAS
Louth, Monaghan, Offaly, Tipperary

FAMILY RANKING
1890: 22nd *1996*: 21st

NO. OF BIRTHS
1890: 386

Famous Names

DONOGH O'CARROLL

Founder of the first Cistercian monastery in Ireland at Mellifont, Co. Louth c. 1145. The family provided no fewer than six abbots of nearby Louth Abbey before its dissolution in 1540.

CHARLES CARROLL (1737–1832)

Charles Carroll, a signatory of the American Declaration of Independence, was one of the old Ely O'Carroll family.

PAUL VINCENT CARROLL (1900–1968)

This Dublin native, a playwright and sharp critic of the Irish clergy and Irish provincial life, was of the same stock. He won the New York Drama Critics' Circle Awards in 1938 and 1939 and, after emigrating to Scotland, was one of the founders of the Glasgow Citizens Theatre.

Casey

HERALDIC BLAZON

Argent a chevron between
three eagles heads erased
gules

Casey, O'Casey and MacCasey come from the Irish *cathasach*, meaning 'vigilant in war', a personal name which was quite common in early Ireland. This, no doubt, accounts for the fact that Ó Cathasaigh arose as a separate surname in at least five distinct areas, in counties Cork, Dublin, Fermanagh, Limerick and Mayo, with Mac Cathasaigh confined to the Louth/Monaghan area. MacCasey is extremely rare today, but in the fourteenth century there were numerous churchmen of the name in the diocese of Clogher. In medieval times generally, the Dublin and Fermanagh Caseys were the most prominent, respectively lords of the Suathni and hereditary abbots (*erenaghs*) of Devenish; their power had been broken by the seventeenth century. The name is rare in Fermanagh now, but is still common in north Co. Dublin to this day, as it is in Mayo and north Connacht generally. However, most present-day bearers of the surname are to be found in Munster, not only in Cork and Limerick, but also in Kerry and Tipperary. The presence of the family is recorded in many placenames, including Ballycaseys in counties Limerick, Galway, Tipperary and Clare.

The arms shown are those of the Co. Limerick sept, part of the great tribe of the Dál gCais, who claimed descent from Cas, a semi-mythical prehistoric figure. The family were based near Bruff in Co. Limerick. The depiction of the eagle, with its legendary ability to look into the sun without blinking, may be connected to one of the old tribal gods of the Dál gCais, Derctheine, the fiery-eyed one.

Famous Names

ADMIRAL JOSEPH GREGORY O'CASEY (1787–1862)

Of Co. Limerick stock, Admiral O'Casey became Minister of the Marine in the government of France.

SEÁN O'CASEY (1880–1964)

One of Ireland's most famous dramatists, Seán O'Casey wrote of the squalor and humanity of the Dublin slums in the early part of the twentieth century, in terms which were critical of nationalist rhetoric. His best plays are *The Shadow of a Gunman* (1923), *Juno and the Paycock* (1924) and *The Plough and the Stars* (1926).

LORD RICHARD GARDINER CASEY (1890–1976)

Governor-general of Australia from 1965 to 1969 and the first life peer to be created outside of the United Kingdom.

BISHOP EAMONN CASEY (b. 1927)

Despite his tireless work for Trócaire, the Irish bishops' Third World relief and development agency, Bishop Casey is likely to be remembered for the controversy which erupted in 1992 when it emerged that while bishop of Kerry he had a liaison with an American woman and had a teenage son.

Cassidy

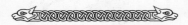

HERALDIC BLAZON

Per chevron argent and gules, in chief two lions rampant and in base a boar passant both counterchanged

In Irish Ó Caiside, 'descendant of Caiside', from Cas, meaning 'curly-headed', the surname is inextricably associated with Co. Fermanagh, where the family were famous for centuries as poets, churchmen, scholars and as hereditary physicians to the great Maguire chieftains. As these occupations attest, unlike many other prominent Irish families they were essentially peaceful; the exploits for which they are recorded in the Annals are healing, poetry and piety. In Fermanagh, their original seat was at Ballycassidy, north of Enniskillen. Two other placenames in the county also record their importance, Cassidy in Derryvullan civil parish, and Farrancassidy in Inishmacsaint. As their healing skills became widely known, many Cassidys were employed by other chiefs, particularly in the north of the country, and the name is now particularly common in counties Donegal, Monaghan and Antrim, as well as in the original homeland of Fermanagh. The final collapse of the old Gaelic order in the seventeenth century left them, like so many others, without their traditional role. Although less numerous elsewhere, the name is now also familiar throughout Ireland, with the smallest numbers to be found in Connacht.

In 1890 141 Cassidy births were recorded, the vast majority in counties Donegal, Antrim and Fermanagh, with a significant number also in Dublin.

TRADITIONAL FAMILY AREAS
Fermanagh

FAMILY RANKING
1890: 146th   *1996*: 141st

NO. OF BIRTHS
1890: 141

Famous Names

GIOLLA MOCHUDA MÓR CAISIDE (d. 1143)

One of the earliest and best-known poets of the family.

WILLIAM CASSIDY (1815–1873)

The grandson of an Irish emigrant, William Cassidy rose to become an eminent American politician.

VIRGINIA CASSIDY

The mother of Bill Clinton, 42nd President of the United States, was Virginia Cassidy, who married Roger Clinton when Bill was four years old.

NEAL CASSIDY (d.1967)

This friend of, and inspiration to, many of the American 'Beatnik' writers of the 1950s, appears under various aliases in the novels of Jack Kerouac.

Clancy

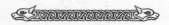

HERALDIC BLAZON
Argent two lions passant
guardant in pale gules

The Irish version of the surname is Mac Fhlannchaidh, from the personal name Flannchadh, which, it is thought, meant 'red warrior'. It originated separately in two different areas, in counties Clare and Leitrim. In the former, where they were a branch of the McNamaras, their eponymous ancestor being Flannchadh Mac Namara, the Clancys formed part of the great Dál gCais tribal group, and acted as hereditary lawyers, or brehons, to the O'Brien chieftains. Their homeland was in the barony of Corcomroe in north Clare, and they remained prominent among the Gaelic aristocracy until the final collapse of that institution in the seventeenth century. The family were prominent in the defence of Limerick in 1691, and many of the name were among the 'Wild Geese' who emigrated to the service of France after defeat. Placenames recording their presence and influence include Ardmaclancy in Kilfinaghta civil parish and Caherclanchy in Dysert.

The Leitrim family of the name were based in the Rosclogher area of the county, around Lough Melvin. Today, the surname is still most common in Leitrim and Clare, with significant numbers also found in the adjacent counties.

DEMOGRAPHIC DATA

TRADITIONAL FAMILY AREAS
Clare, Leitrim

FAMILY RANKING
1890: 232nd *1996*: 202nd

NO. OF BIRTHS
1890: 100

Famous Names

PEADAR CLANCY (1901–1920)

One of three prisoners killed in retaliation for the shooting of British agents on Bloody Sunday in 1920, during the War of Independence.

WILLIE CLANCY (1918–1975)

A native of Milltown Malbay in Co. Clare who was famous country-wide for his skill and warmth as a musician (on pipes, flute, fiddle and whistle). When he died, another piper, Seamus Ennis, said of him, 'He died of a big heart'.

THE CLANCY BROTHERS

Originally from Carrick-on-Suir, Co. Tipperary, The Clancys teamed up with Tommy Makem in the 1950s and played a large part in the revival of traditional Irish music. Although they were part of the international folk music movement, their material drew attention to the Irish originals.

TOM CLANCY (b. 1947)

An American thriller writer who specialises in the inclusion of military and technical detail. His best-known book is *The Hunt for Red October*.

Cleary

HERALDIC BLAZON
Or three nettle leaves vert

Ó Cléirigh, meaning 'grandson of the scribe' is the Irish for both (O')Cle(a)ry and, in many cases in Ireland, Clarke. The surname is of great antiquity, deriving from Cléireach of Connacht, born c. 820, in turn descended from Guaire, a seventh-century king of Connacht. Cléireach derives from the same root as the English 'cleric' and 'clerk' and was used in the same way to describe both a priest and a scholar. Unusually, the anglcisation of the Irish name as Clark was actually quite accurate.

The first of Cléireach's descendants to use his name as part of a fixed hereditary surname was Tigherneach Ua Cléirigh, lord of Aidhne in south Co. Galway, whose death is recorded in the year 916. It seems likely that this is the oldest true surname recorded anywhere in Europe. The power of the family in their original Co. Galway homeland, close to the modern town of Gort, was broken by the thirteenth century, and they scattered throughout the island, with the most prominent branches settling in Derry and Donegal, where they became famous as poets, in Cavan, where many of the bearers appear to have anglicised the name as Clarke, and in the Kilkenny/Waterford/Tipperary region.

In 1890 Clark was ranked 31st most-common surname with 345 births of the name, while Cleary was 171st with 127; by 1996 the rankings were, respectively, 20th and 177th.

DEMOGRAPHIC DATA

TRADITIONAL FAMILY AREAS
Cavan, Derry, Donegal, Galway,
Kilkenny, Tipperary, Waterford

FAMILY RANKING
1890: 31st (Clark), 171st (Cleary)
1996: 20th (Clark), 177th (Cleary)

NO. OF BIRTHS
1890: 345 (Clark), 127 (Cleary)

Famous Names

MICHEÁL Ó CLÉIRIGH (1575–1643)

A member of the literary Donegal sept, he was the prime mover behind
the *Annals of the Four Masters*, the most famous work of Irish historical
scholarship. The tradition of scholarship in the family continued down to
the nineteenth century, when a Dublin antiquarian who had borrowed
the family collection of manuscripts died; the collection was sold as part
of his estate to the Royal Irish Academy, where they remain.

THOMAS CLARKE (1857–1916)

One of the prime movers behind the Easter Rising of 1916 and the first
'signatory' of the Proclamation of Independence. He was summarily
executed immediately after the rebellion.

JULIE AND DESIREÉ CLERY (1857–1916)

The Clery (or Clary) sisters of Marseilles led remarkable lives. Descended
from a Co. Limerick merchant family, they married into the élite of
Napoleonic France. Desireé's husband, Bernadotte, became Charles XIV
of Sweden, while Julie's husband, Joseph Bonaparte, was Napoleon's
younger brother and was at different points king of Naples for two years
and king of Spain for five.

Connolly

HERALDIC BLAZON
Argent on a saltire sable
five escallops of the field

A number of original Irish names have been anglicised as Connolly. The Ó Conghalaigh, from *conghal*, 'as fierce as a wolf', were based in Connacht, where the English version is now often spelt Connelly, or Conneely. The name arose as Ó Coingheallaigh in west Cork, while Ulster Connollys derive from both the Ó Conghalaigh of Fermanagh, who gave their name to Derrygonnelly, 'Connolly's oakwood', and the Monaghan Connollys, for whom a number of separate origins are suggested, such as a branch of the southern Uí Néill, or as a branch of the MacMahons. Whatever their origin, the Monaghan family have been the most well known of the Connollys. They are first noted as coming to prominence in the fifteenth century and are recorded as having Chiefs of the Name up to the seventeenth century. They were instrumental in organising the native Irish rebellion of 1641 and, following its failure, lost their power and possessions.

The variant, Conneely, was found exclusively in Connacht in 1890, with most occurrences in Co. Galway.

Famous Names

WILLIAM CONNOLLY (1662–1729)

Although born in Ballyshannon, Co. Donegal, William Connolly was a member of the Monaghan branch. He amassed enormous wealth by dealing in property confiscated from the native landowners after the defeat of James II at the Battle of the Boyne. He became a pillar of the Anglo-Irish establishment, holding the Speakership of the Irish House of Commons among other appointments. He is best remembered now for Castletown House, the magnificent Palladian mansion he built in Co. Kildare.

JAMES CONNOLLY (1870–1916)

Also of the Monaghan family was the rather different James Connolly, the founder of Irish socialism. Born of Irish emigrant parents in Edinburgh, he came to Ireland in 1913 as a full-time labour organiser and agitator, founded a worker's militia, the Citizen Army, and threw in his lot with the nationalist revolutionaries of 1916. He was the last of the 'signatories' of the Proclamation of Independence to be executed. His writings have become classics of socialist theory.

Costello

HERALDIC BLAZON
Or three fusils azure

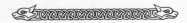

The origin of the surname Costello provides a perfect illustration of the way the native Irish absorbed the invading Normans. Soon after the invasion, the de Angulo family, also known as Nangle, settled in Connacht, where they rapidly became powerful. After only three generations, they had begun to give themselves a surname formed in the Irish manner, with the clan taking Jocelyn de Angulo as their eponymous forebear. Jocelyn was rendered Goisdealbh in Irish, and the surname adopted Mac Goisdealbhaigh, later given the phonetic English equivalent, Costello. Over many generations they carried on a bitter feud, in thoroughly Gaelic fashion, with their rivals in the region, the McDermotts. Their power continued up to the seventeenth century, centred in east Mayo, where they gave their name to the barony of Costello; the centre of their influence was the area around the modern town of Ballaghadereen. Today the surname is widely spread throughout Ireland, with the largest concentrations still in the historic homeland of Connacht.

In Donegal, Costello has also been occasionally used as the anglicisation of Ó Casalaigh, more usually given as Cushley, and in Roscommon Casserley, from the original Mac Casarlaigh, has also at times been rendered as Costello.

In 1890 there were 142 births of the name, mainly concentrated in the four Atlantic counties of Limerick, Clare, Galway and Mayo.

TRADITIONAL FAMILY AREAS
Mayo

FAMILY RANKING
1890: 136th   *1996*: 133rd

NO. OF BIRTHS
1890: 147

Famous Names

JOHN A. COSTELLO (1891–1976)

Taoiseach (Prime Minister) of the Republic of Ireland from 1948 to 1951 and 1954 to 1957. He was responsible for finally taking the country out of the British Commonwealth in 1949.

DECLAN COSTELLO (b. 1927)

The son of John A. Costello was Attorney-General from 1973 to 1977 and was appointed President of the High Court in 1995.

PAUL COSTELLO (b. 1945)

A fashion designer of international repute, and particularly well-known for his use of Irish fabrics.

ELVIS COSTELLO (b. 1950)

The son of Irish parents who emigrated to London, he was born Declan McManus. He is one of the most original and influential songwriters of his generation.

Coughlan

HERALDIC BLAZON
Argent three lions
passant guardant
gules crowned or

Two original Irish versions of Coughlan (and its variants (O')Coghlan, Coglin and Cohalan) exist: Ó Cochláin and Mac Cochláin, both derived from *cochal*, meaning 'cloak' or 'hood'. The Mac Cochláin were part of the great tribal grouping of the Dál gCais, claiming descent from the semi-mythical Cas, which also produced the O'Briens and the McNamaras. Their territory was in the present Co. Offaly, near the modern town of Banagher. They retained a large measure of their influence even after the seventeenth century, with Members of Parliament of the name in 1689 and 1790. As recently as the early nineteenth century the family are recorded as landlords in the area. Shale (Coughlan) in Killoscully parish in Co. Tipperary, near the Offaly border, records their name.

Co. Cork was the homeland of the Ó Cochláin, where the name appears to have arisen in more than one area, with mention of the name in the Blackwater valley region and in a territory near the modern town of Mallow. The strongest historical association of the name in Cork, however, is with the baronies of East and West Carbery, and Barrymore, and particularly with the Schull-Kilmore district of west Cork. The name is now common throughout west Cork. Interestingly, the surname tends to be pronounced differently in different areas of Co. Cork, as 'Cocklin' in the west and 'Cawlin' in the east.

```
DEMOGRAPHIC DATA

TRADITIONAL FAMILY AREAS
Cork, Offaly

FAMILY RANKING
1890: 172nd   1996: 165th

NO. OF BIRTHS
1890: 125
```

Famous Names

EUGENE ('EUDIE') COUGHLAN (b. 1900)

One of Cork's most famous hurlers, having won All-Ireland medals in
1919, 1926, 1928, 1929 and 1931. In 1985 he won an All-Time
All-Star award.

EAMONN COUGHLAN (b. 1952)

The world's top middle-distance indoor runner from the mid-1970s to
the mid-1980s, setting six world indoor records and winning the World
Championship 5000 metres in 1983. In 1994 he became the first athlete
over 40 years of age ever to run a mile in under four minutes.

Crowley

HERALDIC BLAZON

Argent a boar passant
azure between three
crosses crosslet gules

In form Crowley is English, a habitation name from an Old English term meaning 'wood of the crows', and no doubt some of those in Ireland bearing the name derive from English stock. However, the vast majority are of Gaelic Irish extraction, with Crowley an anglicisation of Ó Cruadhlaoich, from *cruadh* and *laoch*, meaning 'hardy' and 'warrior'. The Cruadhlaoch from whom the family take their name lived in the mid-eleventh century and was in fact one of the MacDermots of Moylurg in Connacht, Diarmuid an Cruadhlaoch, a son of Conchubhar son of Diarmuid, a quo the Mac Diarmuida Ruaidh, MacDermott Roe. Some time later, probably in the late thirteenth century, descendants of an Cruadhlaoch migrated from Connacht to Co. Cork, where they settled an area north of the Bandon river in the barony of East Carbery. A local tradition has it that they acquired their territory by marrying into the ruling family of the Coughlans, whom they then ousted. The townlands of Curraghcrowly East and West in this district record their presence.

In any event, while the original Connacht branch of the family declined, descendants of the Cork family prospered and multiplied, in part no doubt due to their well-deserved and formidable reputation as fighters. Their dispossession in the confiscations of the seventeenth century was almost total, since they were prominent on the losing sides in all the major conflicts of the period. The vast majority of Irish Crowleys today are connected to the Cork branch, and that county is still home to most of them.

Of the 161 births of the name in 1890, 116 were in Co. Cork.

TRADITIONAL FAMILY AREAS
Cork

FAMILY RANKING
1890: 121st *1996*: 138th

BIRTHS
1890: 161

Famous Names

NICHOLAS JOSEPH CROWLEY (1819–1857)

Nicholas Joseph Crowley was a distinguished portrait painter.

EUGENE CROWLEY (b. 1926)

This native of Ballineed, Co. Cork, was Commissioner of the Gárda
Síochána from 1988 to 1991.

BOB CROWLEY (b. 1955)

Another Corkman, this time with an international reputation as a stage
designer. He works with the National Theatre and Royal Shakespeare
Company in Britain.

Cullen

HERALDIC BLAZON
Gules on a chevron between
three dexter hands erect
couped at the wrist argent
a garb of the first between
two trefoils slip vert

The surname Cullen may be of either Norman or Gaelic origin. The Norman name has been derived both from the city of Cologne in Germany, and from Colwyn in Wales, and was originally Colyn. In Ireland this Norman family was prominent principally in Co. Wexford, where their seat was at Cullenstown castle in Bannow parish. In the Cromwellian confiscations of the seventeenth century the lands and castle were given to the Boyse family. The remains of the castle are still to be seen.

Much more numerous in modern times, however, are descendants of the Ó Cuilinn, a name taken from *cuileann*, meaning 'holly-tree'. The more than 150 Irish placenames which include 'cullen' are much more likely to derive directly from the original word than from the family name. The name originated in south-east Leinster, where the family were powerful before the ascendancy of the O'Tooles and the O'Byrnes in the fourteenth century, and this area has remained their stronghold, with the majority to be found even today in counties Wicklow and Wexford.

Several other Gaelic originals have also sometimes been anglicised as Cullen. The Ó Cuileamhain, also based in south Leinster, are more usually anglicised Culloon or Culhoun, while the Mac Cuilin of Leitrim are normally found as McCullen or McQuillan.

Famous Names

JOSÉ MARIA CULLEN

This descendent of the Cullens of Lisbigny, Co. Offaly was provincial governor of Buenos Aires in the nineteenth century.

CARDINAL PAUL CULLEN (1803–1878)

The first Irish cardinal, he presided over, and guided, the revival of the power of the Catholic Church in nineteenth-century Ireland He was one of the founders of what is now University College Dublin.

SIR WILLIAM PORTUS CULLEN (1855–1935)

One of many young Irish emigrants to Australia who gained high office in their adopted land; he became Chief Justice of New South Wales. *Eucalyptus Cullenii* is named after him.

FATHER JAMES ALOYSIUS CULLEN (1841–1921)

Another immensely influential churchman, the founder of the *Irish Messenger* in 1888 and the Pioneer Total Abstinence Association in 1898. At their height, the Pioneers had a membership of over 300,000.

Daly

HERALDIC BLAZON
Per fess argent and or a lion
rampant per fess sable and
gules, in chief two dexter
hands couped at the wrist
of the last

The surname (O')Daly (and its variants Daily, Daley, etc.) is Ó
Dálaigh in Irish, deriving from *dálach*, 'one who is present at
assemblies'; the root word is Dáil, now the official title of the
Republic of Ireland's parliament. A connection is possible between
the meaning of the name and the long tradition of scholarship associated with those who bear it, since the *ollamh* of Gaelic Ireland had
a place of honour at the tribal *dáil* as a man of learning and a poet.

Medieval genealogists derived the family from the southern Uí
Néill, part of the tribal grouping that also produced the O'Donnells
and the O'Neills, and located their homeland in the present Co.
Westmeath. Cuchonnacht Ó Dalaigh, head of a famous bardic school
in neighbouring Meath, is the first clearly historical individual to
appear in these genealogies. He died in 1139, and his grandson Aengus
is credited as the progenitor of the various family branches which
spread through the country by acting as *ollaimh* to the most prominent
families – the MacCarthys of Munster, the O'Connors of Connacht,
the O'Byrnes of Leinster, the O'Loughlins of Clare and others.

Although the name's Westmeath origin is best known, from a very
early date families of the name were prominent in Co. Cork, especially in the area around the peninsula of Muintervarra or Sheep's
Head in the west. The likeliest explanation is that the name had a
separate origin in the south. Even so, the O'Dalys of Desmond had
an equally strong association with poetry and learning: so potent
were the poems of Aonghus Ó Dalaigh of Ballyroon that he was
murdered by one of the victims of his satires.

DEMOGRAPHIC DATA

TRADITIONAL FAMILY AREAS
Cork, Westmeath

FAMILY RANKING
1890: 24th   *1996*: 28th

NO. OF BIRTHS
1890: 203

Famous Names

CEARBHALL Ó DALAIGH (1911–1978)

The fifth president of Ireland and a man of wide learning and culture. He was a noted linguist, and also served as Chief Justice of the Supreme Court.

CARDINAL CATHAL (b. 1917)

The former Roman Catholic Primate of All Ireland, Cardinal Cathal Daly is also a distinguished scholar.

RICHARD J. DALY (1920–76)

The mayor of Chicago for 21 consecutive years from1955. Control over his Democratic 'machine' in America's 'Second City' made him one of the most influential and notorious party managers of his generation.

Dempsey

HERALDIC BLAZON
Gules a lion rampant argent,
armed and langued azure
between two swords points
upwards of the second
pommels and hilts or one in
bend dexter the other in
bend sinister

In the original Irish Dempsey is Ó Diomasaigh, from *diomasach*, meaning 'proud'. The name was also occasionally anglicised as Proudman. The Ó Diomasaigh originated in the territory of Clanmalier, on the borders of what are now counties Laois and Offaly, and remained powerful in the area until the seventeenth century. In the 12th century, O'Dempsey, Chief of Offaly, was one of the few native Irish leaders who defeated Strongbow. In later years, their allegiance was to the English and they were involved with the newcomers in the massacre of the O'Lalors in Laois in 1577, an action which local tradition says was responsible for their later losses. James I recognised the strength of the family by granting the title 'Viscount Clanmalier' to Terence Dempsey. The loyalty of the family to the Crown was short-lived, however, and the Williamite wars later in the century destroyed their power and scattered them. The surname is now found throughout the country. It is recorded in the placename Knocknadempsey, in Neddans civil parish in South Tipperary. In Ulster, Dempsey is common in Co. Antrim, where it may be a version of 'Dempster', a Scottish name meaning 'judge', or possibly an anglicisation of Mac Diomasaigh, also sometimes rendered as 'McGimpsey'.

In 1890 recorded births of the name showed particular concentrations in Antrim, Cork and Wexford.

DEMOGRAPHIC DATA

TRADITIONAL FAMILY AREAS
Antrim, Offaly, Laois

FAMILY RANKING
1890: 192nd   *1996*: 164th

NO. OF BIRTHS
1890: 117

Famous Names

WILLIAM HARRISON (JACK) DEMPSEY (1895–1983)

Better known as Jack Dempsey, one of the most popular heavyweight boxing champions of all time. He was born in Manassa, Colorado, and his ferocious attacking style earned him the nickname 'the Manassa Mauler'. He was world champion from 1919 to 1926, when he lost the title to Gene Tunney.

JEREMIAH DEMPSEY (b. 1906)

The guiding spirit behind the Irish national airline, Aer Lingus, from its foundation in 1937 until his retirement in 1967. He was President of the IATA in 1962.

NOEL DEMPSEY (b. 1945)

A prominent member of the Fianna Fáil political party for many years, and minister of state in a number of governments.

Dillon

HERALDIC BLAZON
Argent a lion passant
between three crescents
gules

In Ireland Dillon may be of Gaelic or Norman origin, the former from Ó Duilleáin, possibly from *dall*, meaning 'blind', the latter from de Leon, from the place of the same name in Brittany. This, of course, accounts for the lion in the family arms. The Norman family have been prominent in Ireland since the arrival of their ancestor Sir Henry de Leon in 1185. He was granted vast estates in counties Longford and Westmeath, and his descendants retained their power up to modern times, with Co. Westmeath becoming known simply as 'Dillon's Country'. Among the many titled members of the family were Baron Drumraney, the Earls of Roscommon, the Lords of Clonbrock in Galway, Viscount Dillon and the French Counts Dillon. Another branch of the family settled in Co. Mayo, where they are still well known today. After the Williamite wars of the seventeenth century, many members of the family served in continental regiments, especially the army of France, a tradition which continued down to the nineteenth century. There are many Dillons in France today.

The surname is sometimes confused with Dillane, from the Irish Ó Duilleáin, a north Kerry/Limerick name more usually anglicised as Delane.

Famous Names

EILÍS DILLON (b.1920)

A prolific novelist, playwright and author of children's books.

WENTWORTH DILLON (1633–84)

The 4th Earl of Roscommon, he spent most of his life in the literary salons of Restoration London and was buried in Westminster Abbey.

SIR JAMES DILLON (d. 1669)

The founder of 'Dillon's Regiment', the best-known Irish regiment in the French army. He had been a Member of Parliament for Wicklow from 1639 to 1642 and was forced to flee to France after the invasion of Cromwell. He died in 1669, a Field Marshal of France.

DILLON POLITICANS

Many Dillons have been distinguished politicians, including John Talbot Dillon (1740–1805), Member of Parliament for Wicklow; John Blake Dillon (1816–66), founder of the *Nation* newspaper and later Member of Parliament for Tipperary; his son, also John Blake Dillon (1851–1927), Member of Parliament in Parnell's party; and his grandson James Dillon (1902–86), twice Minister for Agriculture after independence.

Doherty

HERALDIC BLAZON

Argent a stag springing
gules, on a chief vert
three mullets of the first

Doherty and its many variants – (O')Dogherty, Docherty, Dougharty etc. – comes from the Irish Ó Dochartaigh, from *dochartach*, meaning 'unlucky' or 'hurtful'. The original Dochartach from whom the clan descend, lived in the tenth century and has traditionally been claimed as twelfth in lineal descent from Conall Gulban, son of Niall of the Nine Hostages, progenitor of the great tribal grouping of the Uí Néill. Conall gave his name to the territory he conquered, Tir Chonaill, the Irish for Donegal, and to the sub-group of the Uí Néill, the Cineal Chonaill, the race of Conall, the collective name for the many families which claim descent from him, such as the Gallaghers and the O'Donnells, as well as the Dohertys. The original homeland of the O'Dohertys was in the barony of Raphoe in Co. Donegal, with the chief seat at Ardmire in the parish of Kilteevoge.

In the twelfth century, the family became kings of Tirconnell, and virtually without interruption ruled Inishowen for almost five hundred years, until the defeat and execution of Sir Cahir O'Doherty at the start of the seventeenth century. Seán O'Doherty, Cahir's brother, managed to survive and some of his family made their way to Catholic Spain in the eighteenth century. His descendant, Dr Ramón Salvador O'Doherty, lives in Cadiz. In 1989 he was recognized as Chief of the Name by the Chief Herald of Ireland.

In 1890 almost two-thirds of the recorded surnames were found in Ulster, mostly in Donegal and Derry.

DEMOGRAPHIC DATA

TRADITIONAL FAMILY AREAS
Donegal

FAMILY RANKING
1890: 13th   *1996*: 14th

NO. OF BIRTHS
1890: 457

Famous Names

CHARLES JOSEPH DOHERTY (1855–1931)

Minister of Justice in the Canadian government, he represented his country at the League of Nations.

KEVIN O'DOHERTY (1823–1905)

Kevin O'Doherty divided his adult life between Ireland and Australia. After serving a sentence of transportation in Tasmania for his writings at the time of the Young Ireland uprising, he returned to complete his medical studies in Dublin. After qualifying he set off for Brisbane and became a member of the Queensland Legislature. On an extended visit to Ireland in the 1880s he also became Member of Parliament for North Meath.

Donnelly

HERALDIC BLAZON

Argent two lions rampant combatant supporting a dexter hand couped apaumée gules, in the base the sea therein a salmon naiant proper

Donnelly is Ó Donnghaile in Irish, from Donnghal, a personal name made up of *donn*, meaning 'brown' and *gal*, meaning 'bravery'. The original ancestor was Donnghaile Ó Néill, who died in 876, himself a descendant of Eoghan, son of Niall of the Nine Hostages, the fifth-century king who supposedly kidnapped St Patrick to Ireland. The family were thus part of the great northern tribal grouping, the Cenel Eoghain. Their territory was first in Co. Donegal, but they later moved eastwards into Co. Tyrone, where the centre of their power was at Ballydonnelly. Many of the family were hereditary bards, but their chief historical fame is as soldiers, especially in the wars of the seventeenth century. Donnell O'Donnelly, one of the best known of the family, died at the battle of Kinsale in 1602. Patrick Modardha O'Donnelly managed to re-take Ballydonnelly castle from Lord Caulfield in the rising of 1641, but it was lost again, and renamed Castle Caulfield.

A separate family, the Ó Donnghalaigh, appear in the records in the barony of Lower Ormond in Co. Tipperary in the Middle Ages but history appears to have been unkind to them; very few of the name remain in the area.

The name was ranked 67th most common in 1890 and 54th overall in 1996; while only 98th in the Republic, it was 27th in Northern Ireland, reflecting its northern origins. Similarly, placenames reflecting the family presence are exclusively northern, with two **Ballydonnellys** and a **Killydonnelly** in Antrim, **Killdonnelly** in **Monaghan**, and **Donnellystown** in Louth.

TRADITIONAL FAMILY AREAS
Tyrone

FAMILY RANKING
1890: 67th *1996*: 54th

BIRTHS
1890: 240

Famous Names

CHARLES DONNELLY (1914–1937)

One of the most promising of the group of young writers emerging in the mid-1930 who was killed fighting in the International Brigade in the Spanish Civil War at the age of 22.

DERVILLA DONNELLY

One of Ireland's most distinguished scientists. She is professor of Phytochemistry at University College Dublin and was elected president of the Royal Dublin Society in 1981.

Donovan

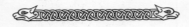

HERALDIC BLAZON
Argent issuing from the sinister side of the shield a cubit dexter arm vested gules cuffed of the first the hand grasping a scian in pale the blade entwined with a serpent all proper

The surname O'Donovan comes from the Irish Ó Donndubhain, from *donn*, 'brown' and *dubh*, 'black' or 'dark', the surname thus meaning 'descendant of the dark brown (-haired/complexioned) man'. The original Donnduban from whom the surname derives was king of the Uí Chairpre in what is now east Limerick and died in 980. In the late twelfth century, as a result of the vicious struggle between the MacCarthys and the O'Briens for dominance in Munster, the O'Donovans were forced to migrate into the neighbouring county of Cork. There they gave the name of their kingdom to the modern barony of Carbery. Their territory comprised a large portion of this area reaching from the south-east coast almost as far as the modern town of Bantry. Their principal seat was at Castledonovan, in the centre of Drimoleague parish.

The family remained powerful and prominent in the area down to the seventeenth century, when they played an important role in the defence of the Catholic and Gaelic Irish in the Cromwellian and Williamite campaigns. Like so many other members of the native aristocracy, the chiefs of the family were dispossessed in the punitive confiscations of the end of that century, but Colonel Daniel O'Donovan, the head of the family at that time, managed to regain some property in the area after the Treaty of Limerick, and re-established the family seat at Bawnlahan in the parishes of Myross and Castlehaven. From him descends the current Chief of the Name, Daniel O'Donovan of Hollybrook, Skibbereen, Co. Cork, The O'Donovan, recognised as such by the Chief Herald of Ireland.

TRADITIONAL FAMILY AREAS
Cork

FAMILY RANKING
1890: 68th   *1996*: 66th

BIRTHS
1890: 222

Famous Names

JOHN O'DONOVAN (1809–1861)

Founder of the Irish Archaeological Society. He virtually single-handedly laid the foundation for all subsequent study of Irish genealogy, history, language and topography.

EDMUND O'DONOVAN (1844–1883)

John O'Donovan's son had a varied career as a journalist and soldier in various foreign armies.

JEREMIAH O'DONOVAN ROSSA (1831–1915)

A leading member of the Fenians and the Irish Republican Brotherhood. After being released from prison he went to the US in 1871, but later returned to Ireland. His funeral oration, delivered by Patrick Pearse, is famous as a statement of the continuity of nationalist tradition.

HARRY O'DONOVAN (1896–1973)

Harry O'Donovan teamed up as a scriptwriter with Jimmy O'Dea, Ireland's best-known comedian from the 1930s to the 1960s, and is best remembered for decades of Dublin pantomimes.

Dowd

HERALDIC BLAZON
Vert a saltire or, in chief
two swords in saltire points
upwards the points
surmounted of the sinister
argent pommels and hilts or

The original Irish name was Ó Dubhda, from *dubh*, or 'black'. In traditional genealogies, the family is one of the Uí Fiachraigh, a large tribal grouping tracing its origin back to Fiachra, brother of Niall of the Nine Hostages, in the fifth century. The O'Dowds were the most powerful in this group, and for centuries their territory including large parts of north-west Mayo and west Sligo, in particular the baronies of Erris and Tirawley in Mayo and Tireragh in Sligo. The Norman invasion of the 13th century curtailed their power, but they retained many of their possessions and much of their influence down to the seventeenth century, as witnessed by the number of O'Dowd bishops of Killalla from the 14th to the 16th centuries. As late as the eighteenth century, a common toast in the Ballina area of Mayo was 'Súil Uí Dhubhda le Árd na Rioch!', a reference to the O'Dowd hopes of regaining their ancestral possession of Ardnaree. The last traditional chief of the family was killed at the Battle of the Boyne in 1690, and is said to have been almost seven feet tall, great stature having always been a feature of the O'Dowds. The name is still most numerous today in the Sligo/Mayo district.

At the end of the nineteenth century, the vast majority of bearers, by a proportion of four to one, were 'Dowd' rather than 'O'Dowd'. A large-scale resumption of the 'O' since then has reversed the statistics.

The name also seems to have arisen separately in two other areas: in Munster the anglicisations 'Doody' and 'Duddy' are frequent in Kerry; and in Derry, where the anglicisation is almost always 'Duddy'.

DEMOGRAPHIC DATA

TRADITIONAL FAMILY AREAS
Mayo, Sligo

FAMILY RANKING
1890: 287th *1996*: 252th

BIRTHS
1890: 84

Famous Names

DAN O'DOWD (1903–1989)

Dan O'Dowd was a Dublin uilleann piper and pipe-maker who is best
remembered for his role in keeping the spirit of traditional music
alive in the capital.

Dowling

HERALDIC BLAZON
Argent a holly tree eradicated proper, on a chief azure a lion passant between two trefoils slipt or

Although it may sometimes appear as a variant of 'Dolan', in most cases Dowling has a separate origin. In form the name is English, derived from the Old English *dol*, meaning 'dull' or 'stupid', but in Ireland it is generally an anglicisation of the Irish Ó Dunlaing. The original territory of the Ó Dunlaing was in the west of the present Co. Laois, along the banks of the River Barrow, which was known as Fearrann ua nDunlaing, 'O'Dowling's country'. The leading members of the family were transplanted to Tarbert in Co. Kerry in 1609, along with other leaders of the 'Seven Septs of Laois', but the surname remained numerous in its original homeland, and spread south and west into Carlow, Kilkenny, Wicklow and Dublin, where it is now very common. As a first name Dunlang was popular in early medieval times in Leinster, where it was also anglicised as Dudley.

In 1890 109 births of the name were recorded, with 84 of these in Leinster, and most of these in Dublin. The other principal focus for the name at that time was in Co. Kilkenny. The influence of the family is recorded in the placenames of Leinster: there are three Ballydowling townlands in Wickow, as well as a Dowling townland in Kilkenny.

DEMOGRAPHIC DATA

TRADITIONAL FAMILY AREAS
Laois

FAMILY RANKING
1890: 207th   *1996*: 224th

BIRTHS
1890: 109

Famous Names

THADY DOWLING (1544–1628)

There is a long tradition of literary work among the Dowlings: Thady
Dowling was well known as a grammarian and historian.

VINCENT DOWLING (1787–1844)
AND FRANK LEWIS DOWLING

Vincent Dowling founded and edited *Bell's Life* and *Firstiana* for almost
thirty years. His work was carried on by his son, Frank Lewis Dowling.

BARTHOLEMEW DOWLING (1823–1863)
AND WILLIAM DOWLING (1828–1880)

These brothers from Co. Kerry were both well-known literary men. The
former wrote *The Brigade of Fontenoy*, while the latter emigrated to
America.

DR JEREMIAH DOWLING (1830–1906)

Author of *The Claddagh Boatman*.

JOE DOWLING (b. 1948)

One of Ireland's leading theatre directors. He was artistic director of
the Abbey Theatre from 1979 to 1985 and has worked with numerous
theatre companies in North America.

Doyle

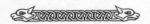

HERALDIC BLAZON

Argent three bucks heads erased gules attired or, within a border compony counter compony or and azure

This name, one of the most common in Ireland, derives from the Irish Ó Dubhghaill, from *dubh*, 'dark', and *gall*, 'foreigner', a descriptive formula first used to describe the invading Vikings, and in particular to distinguish the darker-haired Danes from fair-haired Norwegians. The common Scottish names 'Dougall' and 'MacDougall' come from the same source, and reflect the original pronunciation more accurately. In Ulster and Roscommon, these names now exist as 'McDowell' and 'Dowell', carried by the descendants of immigrant Scottish gallowglasses or mercenaries.

Further evidence for a non-Gaelic origin lies in the absence of the family from any of the Gaelic genealogies. It is not until the sixteenth and seventeenth centuries that the name begins to appear frequently in the *Annals*.

The strongest association of Doyle, however, is with south-east Leinster, and counties Wexford, Wicklow and Carlow in particular, though the name is now found everywhere in Ireland. The stag portrayed in the arms is regarded as a symbol of permanence and endurance, a theme reflected also in one of the family mottoes 'Bhi me beich me', 'I was and I will be'.

The surname is extremely numerous and its association with southern Ireland is marked by the fact that, while it remains 9th most common in the Republic of Ireland in 1996, in Northern Ireland it is only 106th.

Famous Names

JOHN DOYLE (1797–1868)

Dubliner John Doyle was a portrait painter who eventually found success as the political cartoonist HB in *Punch* magazine. He was the grandfather of Sir Arthur Conan Doyle.

SIR ARTHUR CONAN DOYLE (1859–1930)

The Scots-born writer was the author of the Sherlock Holmes stories.

JACK DOYLE (1913–78)

This native of Cork was a famous heavyweight boxer, singer, actor and socialite.

THE MILITARY DOYLES

The Doyles of Bramblestown in Kilkenny produced a remarkable series of distinguished soldiers between 1750 and 1850, including no fewer than six major-generals.

Duggan

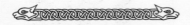

HERALDIC BLAZON

Azure a decrescent argent
between nine estoiles of
eight points or

The Irish Ó Dubhagain, from a diminutive of *dubh*, 'black', is anglicised mainly as Duggan but is also found as Dugan or Doogan, the latter reflecting more accurately the Irish pronunciation. The surname arose simultaneously in a number of areas, including Cork, Roscommon/Galway, Wexford and Fermanagh. The best known family of the name had their territory near the modern town of Fermoy in north Cork, and were originally the ruling family of the Fir Maighe tribal grouping which gave the town its name. They claimed descent from Mug Ruith, the legendary magician of the Fir Bolg. They ceded pre-eminence to the O'Keeffes in the eleventh century, but remained powerful in the area. Along with the other Fir Maighe families they lost their power when the Normans conquered the territory in the twelfth and thirteenth centuries. The family name is found in the parish and townland of Caherduggan in that area.

Another sept of the name is famous in the Uí Maine area of east Galway/south Roscommon largely for producing John O'Dugan (d. 1372), chief poet of the O'Kellys and co-author of the *Topographical Poems*, a long, detailed description of twelfth-century Ireland.

In Wexford, the original Irish name was Ó Duibhghinn, which is also rendered as Doogan and (closer phonetically to the original) Duffin.

DEMOGRAPHIC DATA

TRADITIONAL FAMILY AREAS
Cork, Fermanagh, Galway,
Roscommon, Wexford

FAMILY RANKING
1890: 262nd   *1996*: 245th

NO. OF BIRTHS
1890: 89

Famous Names

PATRICK DUGGAN (1813–1896)

A member of the Galway/Roscommon family who became bishop of Clonfert and is best remembered for his part in the election in Galway in 1872, for which he was tried and acquitted.

AUGUSTINE DUGANNE (1823–1884)

A well known American poet and story writer.

EAMONN DUGGAN (1874–1936)

A nationalist MP in 1918, a signatory to the Anglo-Irish Treaty in 1921 and Minister of Home Affairs in the first Free State government.

NOEL C. DUGGAN (b. 1933)

One of Ireland's best known businessmen. A native of Millstreet, Co. Cork, he has built the Green Glens equestrian centre there into an arena capable of hosting the largest international entertainment events, including the Eurovision Song Contest in 1993.

Dunne

HERALDIC BLAZON
Azure an eagle displayed or

In its form ,'Dunn' is an English surname, from the Old English dunn, 'dark-coloured', and some of the surname in Ireland are undoubtedly of English descent. However, the vast majority of those bearing the name in Ireland descend from the Ó Doinn, from *donn*, used to describe someone who was swarthy or brown-haired. The Ó Doinn first came to prominence as lords of the area around Tinnehinch in the north of the modern Co. Laois (formerly Queen's Co.), and were known as Lords of Iregan up to the seventeenth century. They were especially active in the resistance to the plantations of King's and Queen's Counties in the sixteenth century. At that time the surname was generally anglicised as O'Doyne. Today the name is still extremely common in that part of Ireland, though it is now also widespread throughout the country, with particular concentrations in Leinster.

Perhaps because of the stronger English influence, in Ulster the name is generally spelt Dunn, while it is almost invariably Dunne in other parts. In addition to the English connection, there was also a family of the name among the 'riding clans' along the Scottish border, many of whom settled in Fermanagh after the clans were broken in 1603.

DEMOGRAPHIC DATA

TRADITIONAL FAMILY AREAS
Laois

FAMILY RANKING
1890: 26th   *1996*: 26th

NO. OF BIRTHS
1890: 364

Famous Names

GILLANANAOMH Ó DUINN (1102–1160)

In his day, a celebrated poet and historian.

FINLAY PETER DUNN

Irish-American writer famous for the humourous 'Mr. Dooley' books he published between 1898 and 1919.

JOSEPH DUNN (1930–1996)

The founder and guiding spirit of Radharc Films, a maker of impassioned and committed documentaries on Irish television for thirty years. Among his published works are *No Tigers in Africa* (1986), *No Lions in the Hierarchy* (1994) and *No Vipers in the Vatican* (1996).

LEE DUNNE (b. 1934)

A Dublin novelist, playwright and scriptwriter best known for *Goodbye to the Hill* (1965) and *A Bed in the Sticks* (1968), his first two novels.

SEÁN DUNNE (1956–1995)

One of Ireland's best-known younger poets, particularly identified with Cork and Munster generally, before his untimely death.

Dwyer

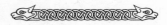

HERALDIC BLAZON
Argent a lion rampant
gules between three
ermine spots

In Irish the surname is Ó Duibhir or Ó Dubhuidhir, made up of *dubh*, meaning 'dark' or 'black' and *odhar*, meaning 'tawny' or 'sallow'. The resumption of the 'O' prefix has now made 'O'Dwyer' much the most common version. In 1890 less than 14% of births were recorded as 'O'Dwyer', while in 1996 it had reached almost 65%. Their original homeland was in the mountains of west Tipperary, at Kilnamanagh between the modern town of Thurles and the Limerick border, where they held power and resisted the encroachments of the English down to modern times. The surname is still extremely common in this area, but Dwyers and O'Dwyers have now also spread into the neighbouring counties of Limerick, Cork and Kilkenny. There is also now a significant settlement of O'Dwyers in Co. Kerry, where the townland of Ballydwyer in Ballymacelligot parish records their influence.

The book *The O'Dwyers of Kilnamanagh* (1933), the best history of the family, was written by Sir Michael O'Dwyer, prominent in the Indian civil service for many years. He was held politically responsible for the massacre of Amritsar in 1919 and was assassinated in London by an Indian nationalist in 1940.

TRADITIONAL FAMILY AREAS
Tipperary

FAMILY RANKING
1890: 124th   *1996*: 94th

NO. OF BIRTHS
1890: 155

Famous Names

JOSEPH O'DWYER (1841–1898)

A doctor in the US, famed for his innovations in diphtheria treatment.

WILLIAM O'DWYER

Another Irish-American, this time an emigrant labourer who went on to become mayor of New York and US ambassador.

MICHAEL DWYER (1771–1825)

The most famous bearer of the name in modern times. He took part in the 1798 rising against the English, and continued his resistance single-handed up to 1803. He was transported to New South Wales, and became High Constable of Sydney.

FATHER EDWARD O'DWYER (1842–1917)

A distinguished Roman Catholic Bishop of Limerick.

MICK O'DWYER (b. 1936)

Gaelic football's most successful coach. After a career which brought him four All-Ireland medals, he went on as coach to lead Kerry to eight All-Ireland championships between 1975 and 1986.

Egan

HERALDIC BLAZON
Quarterly: 1st a tower argent supported on either side by a man in complete armour each holding in the interior hand a battle-axe all proper, in chief a snake fessways or; 2nd and 3rd, Or on a bend vert three plates; 4th, As first quarter but on the tower a swan proper

Egan in Irish is MacAodhagáin, from a diminutive of the personal name Aodh, meaning 'fire', which was anglicised as Hugh, for some strange reason. As well as Egan, Aodh is also the root of many other common Irish surnames, including O'Higgins, O'Hea, Hayes, McHugh, McCoy, etc. The MacAodhagáin originated in the Uí Maine territory of south Roscommon/ east Galway, where they were hereditary lawyers and judges (brehons) to the ruling families. Over the centuries, however, they were dispersed southwards, settling mainly in north Munster and east Leinster, in what are now counties Tipperary, Offaly and Kilkenny. In these areas they continued their hereditary calling, acting as brehons to the Gaelic chiefs; a MacEgan was chief brehon to O'Connor Faly.

In recent years a revival of interest in the family has centred on Redwood Castle in Co. Tipperary, now restored, which was in the possession of Conly MacEgan, a follower of the O'Kennedys, in the mid seventeenth century.

As well as Connacht, their original homeland, they are now most numerous in Leinster, though the surname is now also relatively widespread throughout Ireland. In both Connacht and Leinster the surname has also sometimes been anglicised as Keegan. This variant is most common in north Connacht and in Wicklow.

DEMOGRAPHIC DATA

TRADITIONAL FAMILY AREAS
Galway, Roscommon

FAMILY RANKING
1890: 109th *1996*: 110th

NO. OF BIRTHS
1890: 171

Famous Names

MICHAEL EGAN (1761–1814)

A Franciscan who became the first Roman Catholic archbishop of Philadelphia.

MAURICE FRANCIS EGAN (1852–1924)

Another Philadelphia Egan was Maurice Francis Egan who became professor of English Literature at Notre Dame and went on to have a distinguished career in the US diplomatic corps.

JOHN EGAN (c.1750–1810)

A native of Charleville, Co. Cork, he was a member of Grattan's parliament and opposed the Act of Union. He acquired notoriety as a duelist.

DESMOND EGAN (b. 1936)

This publisher and poet is one of Ireland's best known and most prolific poets, and something of an outsider as one of the very few followers of the Poundian poetic tradition in Ireland. He won the American Society of Poetry award in 1984.

Fahy

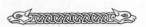

HERALDIC BLAZON
Azure a hand couped at the wrist fessways in chief proper holding a sword paleways in argent pommel and hilt or point downwards pierced through a boar's head erased of the last

Fahy in Irish is Ó Fathaigh, probably from *fothadh*, meaning 'base' or 'foundation'. Another, rarer, English version of the name is Vahey. Strangely, it has also been anglicised as Green because of a mistaken association with *faithce*, meaning 'a lawn' or 'green'. The name still has a very strong association with Co. Galway, where the historic homeland was situated. The area of the family's power was around the modern town of Loughrea in the south of the county, and they retained their property in the region until the catastrophe of the seventeenth century. The surname is still most plentiful in this area, despite the upheavals and migrations which have spread the name quite widely throughout Ireland.

Faithce, 'a green', is a common element in many Irish placenames and, anglicised as '-fahy', it appears in many modern placenames, though it has nothing to do with the family of the same name; the frequency of its occurrence might explain the occasional anglicisation of Ó Fathaigh as Green, however. One place which does record the family name is Fahysvillage in Athenry parish.

In 1890 tmore than half of the the recorded births were in Co. Galway, with particular concentrations also in the adjoining counties of Mayo and Tipperary. As well as Fahy, Green has been used as an anglicisation of other Irish originals, including Ó Grianáin, Mac Glasáin and Mac Giolla Ghlais, either through a phonetic resemblance or a supposed connection with *glas*, meaning the colour green. For this reason and, of course, because many English settlers bore the name, it is now widespread throughout the country.

Famous Names

FATHER ANTHONY FAHY (1805–1871)

This clergyman became famous in his adopted country, Argentina, where the Fahy Institute is named after him.

FRANCIS ARTHUR FAHY (1854–1935),

The best-known bearer of the name was Francis Arthur Fahy, songwriter and literary man, who paved the way for the Irish Literary Revival through his lifelong involvement with the Gaelic League and the London Irish Literary Society.

FRANCIS FAHY (1880–1945)

Francis Fahy played a prominent role in the War of Independence and became *ceann comhairle* (speaker) of the Irish parliament, Dáil Éireann, after independence.

DAVID GREENE (1915–1981)

A senior professor in the School of Celtic Studies in the Dublin Institute for Advanced Studies from 1967 to 1981. He was well known in Irish life for the rigour and vigour of his views.

Farrell

HERALDIC BLAZON
Vert a lion rampant or

As both (O')Farrell and (O')Ferrall, this name in Irish is Ó Fearghail, from the personal name Fearghal, made up of *fear*, 'man', and *gal*, 'valour'. The original Fearghal or Fergal from whom the family claim descent was king of Conmaicne and was killed at Clontarf in 1014. His great grandfather Angall gave his name to the territory they possessed, Annally in Co. Longford. The present name of both the county and the town derives from the family, the full name in Irish being Longphuirt Uí Fhearghaill, or O'Farrell's Fortress. They ruled this area for almost seven centuries, down to the final catastrophes of the seventeenth century, after which many members of the family fought with distinction in the armies of continental Europe. Today the surname is one of the most common in Ireland, with a wide distribution throughout the country, though the largest concentration remains in the historic homeland of Longford and the surrounding areas. In Longford the family's influence is recorded in the placenames, including Lisfarrell (Templemichael parish), Moatfarrell (Clonbroney) and Formoyle Farrell (Rathcline).

The resumption of the 'O' prefix has been noticeably less widespread for this family than for others: 6% recorded the name as 'O'Farrell' in 1890, and 14% in 1996.

TRADITIONAL FAMILY AREAS
Longford

FAMILY RANKING
1890: 41st   *1996*: 31st

NO. OF BIRTHS
1890: 311

Famous Names

CEADAGH O'FARRELL (d. 1690)

One of the leaders of the Annaly O'Farrells, Ceadagh, was killed at the Battle of the Boyne in 1690. Three of his sons fought in the Irish Brigade in the French army and settled in northern France, in Picardy, where the name is still well known.

MICHAEL FARRELL (1899–1962)

Michael Farrell spent almost thirty years writing his novel, *Thy Tears Might Cease*, which remained unfinished at his death. Edited by Monk Gibbon, it achieved international recognition when it was finally published in 1963.

BRIAN FARRELL (b. 1929)

Associate Head of Politics at University College Dublin, and Ireland's best known current-affairs broadcaster for over twenty years, He is now Director-General of the Institute for European Affairs.

MICHAEL FARRELL (b. 1940)

One of Ireland's most accomplished contemporary artists. His nude self-portraits are particularly well known.

Finnegan

HERALDIC BLAZON

Gules two lions rampant
combatant argent supporting
a sword in pale blade wavy
point upwards proper

In Irish Finnegan is Ó Fionnagáin, from Fionnagán, a diminutive of the popular personal name Fionn, meaning 'fairhaired'. It arose separately in two areas, on the borders of the present north Roscommon and northeast Galway, between the modern towns of Dunmore and Castlerea, and in the territory of Oriel taking in parts of the present counties of Monaghan, Cavan and Louth. Descendants of the Connacht family are still to be found in the ancestral homeland, but the majority of modern Finnegans are descended from the Ulster family, and the name remains particularly numerous in counties Cavan and Monaghan. It is now also common throughout Ireland, with the exception of the southern province of Munster.

A separate family, the Mac Fionnmhacáin of Co. Clare, whose name has more usually been anglicised as Finucane or Kinucane, are also sometimes to be found as Finnegan.

In 1890 the surname was recorded around the two ancestral areas, in the Galway area and in counties Armagh, Cavan, Louth and Monaghan. At that time, it was reported that the spelling Finegan was most popular in Galway, Monaghan and Louth, while Finnegan was more frequent in Armagh and Cavan.

TRADITIONAL FAMILY AREAS
Cavan, Galway, Louth, Meath,
Monaghan, Roscommon

FAMILY RANKING
1890: 197th   *1996*: 176th

NO. OF BIRTHS
1890: 115

Famous Names

MARION FINUCANE (b. 1950)

One of Ireland's best contemporary broadcasters, providing a relaxed and impartial forum in which debate can flow freely. She was Radio Journalist of the Year in 1988.

TIM FINNEGAN

The most famous person of the name is fictional. Tim Finnegan is the central character, if that is not too precise a term, in James Joyce's *Finnegans Wake*. The title comes from an old Dublin ballad.

Fitzgerald

HERALDIC BLAZON
Argent a saltire gules

Fitzgerald is a Norman name, made up of *fi(t)z*, Norman French for 'son of', and Gerald, a personal name of Germanic origin from *geri*, 'spear' and *wald*, 'rule'. The family trace their origin to Walter FitzOther, late-eleventh-century keeper of Windsor Forest; his son Gerald was constable of Pembroke Castle in Wales. Walter, Gerald's son, went with Strongbow in the invasion of Ireland and adopted the surname Fitzgerald. Over the next eight centuries the family became one of the most powerful and numerous in Ireland. The head of the main branch, the Duke of Leinster, known historically as the Earl of Kildare, is Ireland's foremost peer. The power of the Munster branch, the Earls of Desmond, was disrupted in the wars of the sixteenth century, but gave rise to three hereditary titles, in existence since at least 1333, which still survive: the Knight of Kerry, the Knight of Glin, and the White Knight, now a Fitzgibbon. The surname is now common, but remains concentrated in the ancient homeland of the Earls of Desmond, counties Cork, Limerick and Kerry.

The arms of the family are typically Norman: clear and simple, military necessity dictating that Norman arms must be easily recognisable. The red saltire cross also indicates the participation of the family in the crusades of the early Middle Ages.

DEMOGRAPHIC DATA

TRADITIONAL FAMILY AREAS
Cork, Kerry, Limerick

FAMILY RANKING
1890: 34th   *1996*: 38th

NO. OF BIRTHS
1890: 330

Famous Names

LORD EDWARD FITZGERALD (1763–1798)

The best known historical bearer of the name was probably Lord Edward Fitzgerald, twelfth child of the 1st Duke of Leinster, whose sympathy with the republican ideals of the French Revolution led him to take part in the Irish rising of 1798, in which he died. His youth and aristocratic origins made him a popular romantic figure.

DR GARRET FITZGERALD (b. 1926)

In our own times, the most famous bearer of the name is of course Dr Garret Fitzgerald, Minister for Foreign Affairs from 1973 to 1977 and Taoiseach between 1981 and 1987.

Flaherty

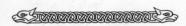

HERALDIC BLAZON
Argent two lions rampant combatant supporting a dexter hand couped at the wrist all gules, in base a boar with eight oars sable

In Irish Flaherty and O'Flaherty are Ó Flaithbheartach, from *flaitheamh*, meaning 'prince' or 'ruler', and *beartach*, meaning 'acting' or 'behaving'. Although the literal translation is 'one who behaves like a prince', a more accurate rendition would be 'hospitable' or 'generous'. The family's original territory was to the east of Lough Corrib in Co. Galway, but the incursions of the Anglo-Normans in the thirteenth century forced them to migrate westwards. From the fourteenth century they controlled the whole of the west of the modern Co. Galway, including Connemara and the Aran Islands, whence the title of their chief, Lord of Iar-Connacht and of Moycullen. Their territory was taken by the Blakes and the Martins in the seventeenth century, but their authority and prestige survived much longer. In 1811 Anthony O'Flaherty was the major tenant, or 'middleman' on the Blake estate at Renvyle in Connemara; a contemporary traveler describes his local status (and his hospitality) in terms which make it clear that he was in effect ruler of the area. Although the name is now common and widespread, the largest number are still to be found in Co. Galway.

A separate family of the same name arose In Donegal, where they were Lords of Aileach at the head of Lough Swilly. In their case, however, the name was anglicised as Lafferty or Laverty. They were driven from Donegal in the 13th century and settled in Co. Tyrone, near Ardstraw. A separate Laverty family in Ulster, mainly based in Co. Antrim, are descended from the Scottish MacLavertys, part of the Clan Donald.

DEMOGRAPHIC DATA

TRADITIONAL FAMILY AREAS
Donegal, Galway, Tyrone

FAMILY RANKING
1890: 265th *1996*: 235th

NO. OF BIRTHS
1890: 88

Famous Names

RODERICK O'FLAHERTY (1629–1718)

The last chief of the family and a celebrated historian. *Iar-Connaught*, his account of west Connacht's early history and families, is still a major source.

MONSIGNOR JAMES O'LAVERTY (1828–1906)

The Co. Down-born author of the renowned *Historical Account of the Diocese of Down and Connor*.

LIAM O'FLAHERTY (1896–1984)

The best known modern bearer of the name. Born on the Aran island of Inishmore, he had a varied career, including a stint with the British Army during the First World War, before settling to writing. He wrote intense psychological dramas (*The Informer*, 1925) and historical novels (*Famine*, 1937), but is best known for his short stories, many of which are among the masterpieces of the genre.

STEPHEN O'FLAHERTY (1902–1982)

The cousin of writer Liam O'Flaherty, he was one of the country's most successful businessmen from the 1940s onwards, as a pioneer of the motor trade.

Flanagan

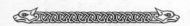

HERALDIC BLAZON
Argent out of a mount in base vert an oak tree proper, a border of the second

In Irish the surname is Ó Flannagáin, a diminutive of *flann*, a personal name which was very popular in early Ireland, and means 'red' or 'ruddy'. Perhaps because of this popularity, the surname arose separately in a number of distinct locations, including counties Roscommon, Fermanagh, Monaghan and Offaly.

In Roscommon they were long associated with the royal O'Connors, traditionally deriving from the same stock, and supplying stewards to the royal household. The centre of their power was between Mantua and Elphin, near the modern town of Castlerea.

In Fermanagh the Flanagans were part of the Cenél Cairbre, the group of families claiming common descent from Cairbre, a son of Niall of the Nine Hostages, the founder of the Uí Néill dynasty. They ruled a large territory covering the west of Lower Lough Erne, and based at Ballyflanagan, now the townland of Aghamore in Magheraboy parish. Today the name is widely distributed throughout Ireland, though the largest concentration remains in the areas of their original homelands, south-west Ulster and north Connacht.

The Monaghan family descend from Flannacán, son of Fogartach King of Farney, whose death is reported in 886. They appear to have been based in the parish of Donaghmoyne.

In Offaly the family lived in the south, in the barony of Ballybritt.

The arms are of the Connacht family and display the royal oak, symbol of the O'Connors, proclaiming their long association with this family, though the tree does not cover the whole shield, a significant difference.

Famous Names

RODERICK FLANAGAN (1828–1861)

An emigrant to Australia, where he founded the *Sydney Chronicle*.

JOHN J. FLANAGAN (1873–1938)

Co. Limerick-born hammer-thrower who won three gold medals in his
sport at the Olympic Games of 1900, 1904 and 1908.

T. P FLANAGAN (b. 1929)

One of the best-known Irish contemporary landscape artists.

FATHER MICHAEL O'FLANAGAN (1876–1942)

A member of the Roscommon family who was prominent in Republican
politics, becoming vice-chairman of Sinn Féin and vice-president of the
Gaelic League.

KEVIN O'FLANAGAN (b. 1919)

One of Ireland's most vesatile sportsmen. He was Irish 100 yards
champion and long jump champion, as well as playing both rugby
and soccer for the Irish national side.

Fleming

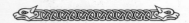

HERALDIC BLAZON
Vair a chief chequy or and
gules

Fleming is an ethnic name simply meaning 'an inhabitant of Flanders'. It is a common surname in Britain, reflecting the importance of the wool trade between England and the Netherlands in the Middle Ages, when many Flemish weavers and dyers settled in England, Wales and southern Scotland. It arrived in Ireland in two ways: following the Norman invasion, when families of the name became prominent in the areas around Dublin; and through the Plantation of Ulster in the seventeenth century, when many Scottish bearers of the name arrived. In Scotland, one Fleming family was part of the Clan Murray, while another family of the name were sheriffs of Lanarkshire and owned a great deal of land there. Today, although widespread elsewhere, the surname is most numerous in Ulster, particularly in counties Antrim and Derry.

In historical terms, the most important Fleming family was one of the earlier southern arrivals, a family that held large tracts of land in counties Meath and Louth down to the seventeenth century, and acquired the title, 'Lords of Slane'. Their espousal of the Jacobite cause led to the loss of all their estates.

TRADITIONAL FAMILY AREAS
Dublin, Louth, Meath

FAMILY RANKING
1890: 110th   *1996*: 134th

NO. OF BIRTHS
1890: 170

Famous Names

NICHOLAS FLEMING

Archbishop of Armagh between 1404 and 1416.

REVEREND RICHARD FLEMING (1542–1590)

This Co. Meath clergyman was an eminent theologian and professor of philosophy at Paris University.

JOHN FLEMING (1815–1895)

A scholar who was prominent in the revival of the Irish language in the nineteenth century.

GEORGE FLEMING (1773–1840)

George Fleming led a notoriously dissolute life as a young man and was forced to flee to France to escape his debts. While there he wrote his memoirs, which caused a great deal of scandal and embarrassment to his former associates in Ireland.

Flynn

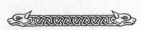

HERALDIC BLAZON
Azure a wolf passant argent,
in chief three bezants

In Irish Flynn and O'Flynn are Ó Floinn, from *flann*, meaning 'reddish' or 'ruddy', which was extremely popular as a personal name in early Ireland. As might be expected, this popularity led to the surname's emergence independently in several areas, including Clare, Cork (two families), Kerry, Mayo, Roscommon, Cavan, Antrim, Fermanagh and Monaghan. The most historically important of these were the families originating in Cork and Roscommon.

One of the Cork families ruled over a territory in Muskerry between Ballyvourney and Blarney down to the twelfth century. Tradition has it that the MacCarthys caused their fall from power. In any case, little is heard of them later. The other Cork family, the Ó Floinn Arda, were so called from the seat of their influence, Ardagh in the parish of Ross in west Cork. By the sixteenth century their authority appears to have waned, though the name remained numerous across Cork.

The Roscommon family were centred on the area in the north of the county around the modern town of Castlerea. The chief enjoyed the dubious right to ride the same horse as the king of Connacht.

In Co. Antrim, the Irish version of the name was Ó Fhloinn, with the initial 'F' silent, so the anglicised version became O'Lynn, or simply Lynn. Other anglicisations include Lind, Linn, Lynd and, occasionally, Lindsay. The O'Lynns ruled the lands between Lough Neagh and the Irish Sea in south Antrim.

DEMOGRAPHIC DATA

TRADITIONAL FAMILY AREAS
Antrim, Cavan, Cork, Kerry, Mayo,
Roscommon

FAMILY RANKING
1890: 39th *1996*: 30th

NO. OF BIRTHS
1890: 319

Famous Names

EDWARD JAMES FLYNN (b. 1845)

Edward James Flynn became Prime Minister of Quebec.

JOHN FLYNN (1880–1951)

A Presbyterian missionary in Australia, and founded the Flying Doctor service, earning him the nickname 'Flynn of the Inland'.

PADRAIG FLYNN (b. 1939)

A member of Dáil Éireann, the Irish parliament, and a minister in five different governments from 1977 until 1993, when he was appointed EU Social Affairs Commissioner.

LIAM O'FLYNN (b. 1945)

Ireland's best known contemporary uilleann piper. He has played with the group Planxty, as a soloist in the orchestral works of Shaun Davey, on film soundtracks and with the American composer John Cage.

Gallagher

HERALDIC BLAZON

Argent a lion rampant sable treading on a serpent in fess proper between eight trefoils vert

In Irish (O')Gallagher is Ó Gallcobhar, from *gall*, meaning 'foreign' and *cabhair*, meaning 'help' or 'support'. The original Gallcobhar from whom the family claim descent was himself sixth in descent from Conall Gulban, son of Niall of the Nine Hostages, the fifth century monarch who was reputedly responsible for the kidnapping of St Patrick to Ireland and who was the founder of the Uí Néill dynasty. The O'Gallaghers claim to be the most senior branch of the Cenél Conaill, the group of families who all descend from Conall Gulban. Their territory was in Tír Chonaill (literally 'Conall's Land'), in what is now Co. Donegal. Despite the claim to seniority, early references to the family are sparse. From the fourteenth to the sixteenth centuries, however, they were hereditary commanders of the cavalry of the forces of the O'Donnell princes of Tir Chonaill.

Today Gallagher is the single most numerous surname in Co. Donegal, and is also very common in the adjoining counties of Derry, Fermanagh and Tyrone. Though less common elsewhere in Ireland, it has spread throughout the country over the centuries. More than thirty variant spellings of the name have been recorded.

TRADITIONAL FAMILY AREAS
Donegal

FAMILY RANKING
1890: 12th *1996*: 20th

NO. OF BIRTHS
1890: 488

Famous Names

REDMOND O'GALLAGHER (1521–1601)

One of the very many O'Gallaghers recorded in Irish church history. He was an enthusiastic supporter of O'Donnell and the other northern lords in their struggle with the English and was killed in that struggle.

WILLIAM DAVIS GALLAGHER (1808–1894)

A well-known American poet whose father had fled Ireland after the failure of the Emmett rebellion of 1803.

PADDY 'THE COPE' GALLAGHER (1873–1964)

A tireless promoter of rural co-operatives, transforming his home town Dungloe in the 1950s and '60s. His nickname came from the local pronunciation of 'co-op'. His son, Pat 'the Cope', is a member of the European Parliament.

RORY GALLAGHER (1949–1995)

Born in Co. Donegal, guitarist Rory Gallagher was raised in Cork. He first became well-known as part of the blues trio Taste in the late 1960s, and went on to become a major blues guitarist with a huge international following.

Hennessy

HERALDIC BLAZON
Vert a stag trippant argent
between six arrows two two
and two saltireways or

The original Irish form of the name is Ó hAonghusa, from the personal name Aongus, still popular as Angus in Scotland, the young god of pre-Christian Celtic tradition. This was quite popular, and it gave rise to the surname in several distinct localities, in the north of the present Co. Offaly, near Kilbeggan from where the family later spread into the adjoining counties of Clare and Tipperary, in southwest Co. Cork, where they formed part of the Corca Laoidhe tribal grouping, descended from pre-Gaelic origins, and in east Cork, in the territory between the present towns of Fermoy and Mitchelstown. The east Cork family produced the most famous bearer of the name, Richard Hennessy (1720–1800) of Ballymacmoy near Mallow, who fought with Dillon's Brigade in the French army, and founded the famous brandy distillery in 1765. This family remain intimately associated with the company, and with Ireland; the present director is Maurice Hennessy, a direct descendant of Richard. The old family home, Ballymacmoy House, was re-purchased by the family in 1932.

Today the surname is still strongly associated with Co. Cork, though significant numbers also appear in counties Limerick, Tipperary and Clare. In the latter area, the name has also been anglicised as Henchy and Hensey.

DEMOGRAPHIC DATA

TRADITIONAL FAMILY AREAS
Cork, Offaly

FAMILY RANKING
1890: 201st *1996*: 198th

NO. OF BIRTHS
1890: 111

Famous Names

SIR JOHN POPE-HENNESSY (1834–1891)

This member of the east Cork family became Member of Parliament for Westmeath in 1859 and went on to a long career as colonial governor in Africa, Asia and the West Indies.

SIR JOHN POPE-HENNESSY (b.1913) AND JAMES POPE-HENNESSY (1916–74)

The grandsons of John Pope-Hennessy have also been well known, the former as writer on art and Professor of Fine Art at New York University, the latter as a journalist and author.

HENRY HENNESSY (1826–1901)

A native of Cork who became professor of Engineering at what is now University College Dublin, professor of Applied Mathematics at the Royal College of Sciences and vice-president of the Royal Irish Academy.

JOHN HENNESSY

John Hennessy, from Bulgaden, Co. Limerick, was the first archbishop of Missouri.

Hickey

HERALDIC BLAZON

Azure a lion passant guardant or, on a chief ermine a bend sable

The original Irish for Hickey is Ó hIcidhe, from *iceadh*, meaning 'healer'. The Hickeys were part of the tribal grouping, the Dál gCais, which produced Brian Ború, the High King of Ireland who defeated the Vikings in 1014. This grouping had its territory in the area now part of Co. Clare and north Tipperary, and it is this area with which the Hickeys remain closely identified. Their surname arose because of their position as hereditary physicians to the royal O'Brien family.

From their original homeland, the name spread first into the neighbouring Co. Limerick, and from there even wider, so that Hickey is today one of the most common and widespread of Irish surnames.

In 1890 the name, had particular concentrations in the old areas of Clare, Limerick and Tipperary, but also in Dublin and Cork.

There has been virtually no resumption of the initial 'O' prefix which has been readopted in other surnames.

TRADITIONAL FAMILY AREAS
Clare, Tipperary

FAMILY RANKING
1890: 151st   *1996*: 116th

NO. OF BIRTHS
1890: 139

Famous Names

JOHN HICKEY (1756–1795) AND THOMAS HICKEY (1760–1822)

The Hickey brothers, John and Thomas, were prominent artists, as a sculptor and a portrait painter respectively.

JOHN D. HICKEY (1911–1977)

A controversial sports journalist with the *Irish Independent* for more than twenty-five years, often at loggerheads with the authorities in charge of Gaelic games.

PATRICK HICKEY (b. 1927)

One of Ireland's most respected painters and printmakers. He was head of painting at the National College of Art and Design from 1986 to 1990.

Higgins

HERALDIC BLAZON

Argent guttée de pois on
a fess sable three towers
of the first

In form, Higgins is an English name, from the medieval given name 'Higgin', a diminutive of 'Hicke', which was in turn a pet form of Richard. In Ireland, however, the vast majority of those bearing the name are of Gaelic Irish stock, Higgins being used as an anglicisation of the Irish Ó hUigín, from *uiginn*, meaning 'Viking'. The original Uigín from whom they claim descent was grandson to Niall of the Nine Hostages, the fifth-century king who founded the powerful tribal grouping the Uí Néill, and they are therefore regarded as part of that grouping. Originally based in the midlands, part of the southern Uí Néill, they moved west over the centuries to Sligo and Mayo, and more than half of those bearing the surname today still live in the western province of Connacht. In Connacht, they achieved fame as poets and scholars.

Famous Names

TADHG DALL Ó HUIGÍN (1550–1591)

One of the most famous Irish poets. He is said to have been killed by the O'Haras, who cut out his tongue in revenge for a satire he had written about them.

FRANCIS HIGGINS (1726–1802)

Francis Higgins is less kindly remembered than Tadhg. A social climber known as 'The Sham Squire', he owned the *Freeman's Journal* and was rumoured to have been paid £1000 to reveal the hiding place of United Irishman Lord Edward Fitzgerald.

DON AMBROSIO O'HIGGINS (1720–1801) AND BERNARDO O'HIGGINS (1788–1842)

Ambrosio O'Higgins became viceroy of Peru for Spain, and his son, Bernardo O'Higgins, is widely revered in South America as the 'Liberator of Chile'. Ambrosio was born in Ballinvary, Co. Sligo, and took the Spanish title Baron de Valenar, Baron Ballinvary.

Hogan

HERALDIC BLAZON
Sable on a chief or three
annulets of the field

The Irish version of the surname is Ó hOgáin, from a diminutive of *óg*, meaning 'young'. The original Ogán from whom the family claim descent lived in the tenth century and was an uncle of Brian Ború, the High King who defeated the Vikings at Clontarf in 1014. Like Brian Ború, they were part of the Dál gCais tribal grouping, whose original territory took in Clare and parts of Tipperary. The (O')Hogans were centred on Ardcrony, near the modern town of Nenagh in north Tipperary, where their chief had his seat. From there, the surname spread far and wide, and is today one of the most common in Ireland, with particular concentrations close to the first homeland, in counties Clare, Tipperary and Limerick. In addition, significant numbers are to be found in Cork, where it is thought that the name may have had a separate origin, in the southwest of that county. Ó hOgáin is recorded as the name of one of the minor families of the Corca Laoidhe tribal grouping.

The family are well represented in the placenames of their original homeland, with two Ballyhogans in north Tipperary (parishes of Knigh and Burgesbeg) and one in south Galway (Abbeygormacan). There is also a Knockhogan in Clare (Doora), a Derryhogan in Tipperary (Twomileborris) and a Drumhogan in Galway (Abbeygormacan).

DEMOGRAPHIC DATA

TRADITIONAL FAMILY AREAS
Cork, Tipperary

FAMILY RANKING
1890: 92nd *1996*: 109th

NO. OF BIRTHS
1890: 193

Famous Names

JOHN HOGAN (1800–1858)

A sculptor who gained an international reputation.

PATRICK HOGAN (1886–1969)

A Labour Party TD and member of Dáil Éireann, the Irish Parliament, for almost forty years. He served as *ceann comhairle* (speaker) from 1951 to 1967.

PATRICK HOGAN (1892–1936)

His namesake was was also a member of Dáil Éireann, the Irish parliament, and became the first Minister for Agriculture after independence.

DESMOND HOGAN (b. 1950)

A native of Ballinalsoe, Co. Galway, and one of the best-known of the young novelists to emerge from the Irish Writers' Co-Op in the 1970s. His stage and television plays and short stories are also highly regarded.

Joyce

Joyce derives from the Breton personal name Iodoc, a diminutive of *iudh*, meaning 'lord', which was adopted by the Normans as Josse. A number of English surnames arose from this Norman original, including Joce, Joass, and Joyce, this last being far more frequent in Ireland than anywhere else.

The first bearer of the name in Ireland was a Thomas de Joise, of Norman Welsh extraction, who in 1283 married Honora, daughter of the O'Brien Princes of Thomond, and settled in west Connacht, on the borders of the modern counties of Mayo and Galway. Their son Mac Mara ('son of the sea') married into the powerful O'Flaherty family and his descendants became completely gaelicised, ruling the area, still known as 'Joyce's Country', until the seventeenth century.

The family were prominent Galway city affairs for four centuries, as one of the 'Fourteen Tribes of Galway', and provided many mayors of the city. One of the most famous symbols of Galway, the Claddagh ring with its heart clasped by two hands, was designed by a Galway silversmith, William Joyce, who learned his trade as a prisoner of 'Barbary' pirates in Algeria at the end of the seventeenth century.

The surname remains strongly associated with the area, with a large majority of Joyces originating in counties Galway and Mayo.

The arms are supposed to originate from the experience of another William Joyce, who took part in the Crusades. On his journey home a mysterious eagle is reputed to have shown him where a vast treasure was buried. On the other hand, the double-headed eagle is a common heraldic symbol of power.

Famous Names

JAMES JOYCE (1882–1941)

Author of *Dubliners, The Portrait of an Artist as a Young Man, Ulysses* and *Finnegans Wake*, was descended from a family who settled in Cork in the eighteenth century. He was acutely aware of the importance of family, and of the antiquity of his own name and of the arms associated with it. In the *Portrait*, Stephen, the central character, tells one of his doubting classmates of the arms registered at Ulster's Office (now the Genealogical Office) and offers to take him there to show them to him. In *Ulysses* Joyce depicts his father shouting 'Head up! Keep our flag flying! An eagle gules volant in a field argent displayed.' In fact the elder Joyce's rallying call was used most frequently to keep spirits up, as the family were forced to abandon yet another home due to unpaid rent. The author's grandmother was an O'Connell from the Iveragh peninsula in Kerry, reputedly of the same family as the politician Daniel O'Connell, the 'Liberator'.

WILLIAM JOYCE (1900–1946)

Known as Lord Haw-Haw, Joyce broadcast Nazi propaganda from Berlin to Britain during the Second World War and was infamous for his introduction to each broadcast: 'Germany calling, Germany calling…' He was subsequently hanged for treason by the British.

Kavanagh

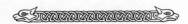

HERALDIC BLAZON
Argent a lion passant gules,
in base two crescents of
the last

Kavanagh, along with its variants Cavanagh, Cavanaugh, etc., is the English version of Caomhanach, one of the very few Gaelic Irish surnames not to include 'O' or 'Mac'. It means 'follower of (St) Caomhan', a name which is itself a diminutive of *caomh*, meaning 'gentle' or 'tender'. It was first borne as a surname in the twelfth-century by Donal, illegitimate son of Dermot MacMurrough, King of Leinster. He became known as Donal Caomhánach through having been fostered by a successor of the saint based probably at Kilcavan in Bannow parish in south Co. Wexford.

Although this Donal was the name's first bearer, in fact the majority of the Kavanagh septs that proliferated from the fifteenth century on descend from Art MacMurrough Kavanagh, King of Leinster, who died in 1418. The Kavanaghs' territory was huge, comprising nearly all of modern Co. Carlow and most of north and north-west Co. Wexford. For good reason was it known as 'the Kavanagh's country': Art held complete control over it, reigning for forty-two years, and even receiving dues from the English crown – the 'black rent', as it was known. The chiefs of the family continued to take the ruling title MacMurrough, but by the start of the seventeenth century their already waning power was broken when English rule was established and north Wexford planted with English settlers.

Despite their loss of power and property, the line of descent from the last duly inaugurated Chief of the Name, Brian Kavanagh, The MacMorrough, remained unbroken to recent times.

DEMOGRAPHIC DATA

TRADITIONAL FAMILY AREAS
Carlow, Wexford

FAMILY RANKING
1890: 48th   *1996*: 50th

NO. OF BIRTHS
1890: 274

Famous Names

ARTHUR MACMURROUGH KAVANAGH (1831–89)

The most extraordinary of the chiefs of the family who became the MacMorrough Kavanagh, Arthur Kavanagh was born without limbs. He also became an artist, poet, adventurer, sailor, father of seven and Member of Parliament for thirteen years.

PATRICK KAVANAGH (1904–1967)

The most famous modern bearer of the name was Patrick Kavanagh, the first poet of modern Ireland to give voice to the realities of life in the new state, as well as being a powerful polemicist.

Keane

HERALDIC BLAZON

Azure on a fess per pale gules and argent between in chief out of the horns of a crescent a dexter hand couped at the wrist and apaumée surmounted by an estoile between on the dexter a horse counter-saliant and on the sinister a lion rampant each also surmounted by an estoile, and in base a salmon naiant all argent, on the dexter side three lizards passant in bend sinister-ways argent and on the sinister an oak tree eradicated vert, over all an escutcheon argent charged with a cross calvary on three grieces proper

Keane and Kane are both anglicisations of Ó Catháin, from a diminutive of *cath*, meaning 'battle'. Keane, however, is much more common in Connacht than in Ulster, the homeland of the majority of the Kanes. This is because Ó Catháin arose separately as a surname in Co. Galway, where the family were a branch of the historic Uí Fiachraigh tribal grouping. Traditionally it has been believed that the prominent Clare Keanes were an offshoot of the Ulster Ó Catháin, but the closeness of Clare and Galway must make this doubtful. In any case, the two forms of the name have been interchangeable for most of Irish history.

The Ulster Ó Catháin were part of the Cenel Eoghain, a loose tribal grouping of the descendants of Eoghan, son of Niall of the Nine Hostages. They originated in the Laggan area of Donegal, and from there moved eastwards in the twelfth century, ousting the O'Connors from north Derry and retaining their lordship of Keenaght and Coleraine until the seventeenth century.

A distinct family, the Ó Céin from Munster, and particularly Co. Waterford, have anglicised their name as Kean(e).

DEMOGRAPHIC DATA

TRADITIONAL FAMILY AREAS
Clare, Derry, Galway, Waterford

FAMILY RANKING
1890: Keane 88th, Kane 96th
1996: Keane 65th, Kane 67th

NO. OF BIRTHS
1890: 202

Famous Names

JOHN B. KEANE (b.1928)

A native of Listowel, Co. Kerry, and one of Ireland's most popular play-wrights. His best-known works include *The Field* (1965), *Big Maggie* (1969) and *Moll* (1972). He has also published three novels.

EDMUND KEAN (1787–1833) AND CHARLES KEAN (1811–1880)

The famous actor Edmund Kean and his son Charles were of the Munster Keans.

MOLLY KEANE (1905–1996)

Another notable member of this family, who published ten novels between 1928 and 1952 under the pen-name M. J. Farrell. She had been largely forgotten by the 1980s, when she re-emerged, writing this time under her own name, and published *Good Behaviour* (1981). Widely regarded as her masterpiece, it is a wickedly witty satire on the decaying world of the Anglo-Irish in which she had grown up.

ROY KEANE (b. 1971)

One of the most talented footballers ever to emerge from Ireland, and played a major role in Manchester United's winning the English football league and cup double in 1994.

Kearney

HERALDIC BLAZON
Argent three lions rampant gules, on a chief azure between two pheons of the first a gauntletted hand fessways or holding a dagger erect proper pommel and hilt or

Kearney is common and widespread in Ireland, and has a number of different origins. In the west it originated in Co. Mayo, near Moynulla and Balla, the territory of the Ó Cearnaigh (from *cearnach*, meaning 'victorious'), where it has sometimes also been anglicised as Carney. A separate family of the same name, but anglicised as (O')Kearney, arose in Clare, and migrated in early times to the area around Cashel in Co. Tipperary. In Ulster the name derives from Mac Cearnaigh, also from *cearnach*; they were part of the Cenél Eoghain, the large group of families descended from Eoghan, son of Niall of the Nine Hostages, the fifth-century monarch who founded the Uí Néill dynasty. The Cearnach from whom they claim descent was a brother of Cosgrach, chief of the Armagh O'Hanlons.

The most important family historically were the Ó Catharnaigh, from *catharnach*, meaning 'warlike'. These were chiefs of a large territory in the midlands, in the modern counties of Meath and Offaly; one of their number became Baron Kilcoursey, from the Offaly placename. An early chief of this family, Tadhg Ó Catharnaigh (d. 1084), became known as An Sionnach, The Fox, and his descendants adopted the name Ó Sionnaigh, which was later anglicised as Fox.

The name's multiple origins can be seen in the many counties with placenames which include it, including Cork (Ballykearney), Down (Kearney village) Kilkenny (Kearneysbay), Louth (Kearneystown) and Kildare (Kearneystown).

DEMOGRAPHIC DATA

TRADITIONAL FAMILY AREAS
Down, Mayo, Tipperary

FAMILY RANKING
1890: 135th   *1996*: 90th

BIRTHS
1890: 147

Famous Names

PEADAR KEARNEY (1883–1942)

A Dubliner and a member of the Irish Republican Brotherhood. He wrote the words of *A Soldier's Song* in 1907 which, after independence, became the Irish national anthem.

ART CARNEY (b. 1918)

A leading American character actor whose long career in television and the cinema peaked in the mid 1970s with an Oscar-winning performance in the film, *Harry and Tonto*

RICHARD KEARNEY (b. 1954)

Professor of philosophy at University College Dublin since 1990. Remarkably precocious and prolific, his work is European rather than Anglo-Saxon in outlook. He has also published poetry and fiction.

Keating

HERALDIC BLAZON

Argent a saltire gules
between four nettle
leaves vert

Although Keating is found as a surname in England, where it derives from the Old English Cyting, from *cyt*, meaning 'kite', in Ireland it is almost always of Norman origin. The town of Keeston in Pembrokeshire got its name from the family and was almost certainly their home in Wales. The family arrived with the Cambro–Norman invaders in the twelfth century and soon became thoroughly Irish, settling in south Leinster, and particularly in Co. Wexford, where the most prominent family were based at Baldwinstown castle. The extent of the family's adoption of Irish ways is vividly illustrated in the descriptions given of them by English writers of the sixteenth and seventeenth centuries: in 1567 the Keatings of Carlow were 'ill-disposed rebels'; in 1562, the Keatings of Wexford were 'out in rebellion and burned many houses'; in 1613 the Keatings of Laois were described as a 'great sept of people'.

The family left their mark also on Irish placenames in the south and east of the country. There are two Keatingstowns in Kilkenny, one Cloghkeating in Limerick and another in Tipperary, and a Ballykeating in north Cork.

The most famous historical bearer of the name was Geoffrey Keating (or Seathrun Céitinn) the poet and historian who lived in the first half of the seventeenth century and wrote *Foras Feasa ar Eireann*, a narrative history of the country defending it against the accounts given by foreign writers..

DEMOGRAPHIC DATA

TRADITIONAL FAMILY AREAS
Wexford

FAMILY RANKING
1890: 167th   *1996*: 184th

NO. OF BIRTHS
1890: 130

Famous Names

PAUL JOHN KEATING (b. 1944)

Paul Keating, of Irish emigrant extraction, was prime minister of Australia from 1991 to 1996. He was first elected to the House of Representatives in 1969, becoming the nation's youngest federal deputy. He served as treasury minister (1983–1991) and deputy prime minister (1990–1991) before ousting Bob Hawke to become Australian Labour Party leader and the country's youngest-ever prime minister in 1991.

SEAN KEATING (1889–1977)

An artist who specialised in traditional scenes, particularly of the Aran Islands, and was president of the Royal Hibernian Academy for fourteen years.

JUSTIN KEATING (b. 1930)

Justin Keating is well-known as a politician, a veterinary surgeon, a lecturer and broadcaster. He was Minister for Industry and Commerce from 1973 to 1979.

Kelly

HERALDIC BLAZON
Azure a tower triple-towered supported by two lions rampant argent, as many chains descending from the battlements between the lions legs or

The surname Kelly comes from the Irish O Ceallaigh, 'grandson of Ceallach', a common personal name which may mean either 'bright-haired' or 'troublesome'. Its popularity meant that it was incorporated into permanent surnames in between seven and ten different places, including Co. Meath, north Wicklow, the Antrim/Derry area, Co. Sligo, Galway/Roscommon, north Down and Co. Laois.

The most prominent of these families are the O'Kellys of Uí Máine, or Hy Many, an ancient territory taking in east Galway and south Roscommon, also known simply as 'O'Kelly's Country'. Their pedigree takes them back to the fifth-century Máine Mór, first chief of the area bearing his name. His descendant, Ceallach, (d. c. 874) was the twelfth chief, and it is from him that the surname derives. His great-great-grandson Tadhg Mór, who died at the Battle of Clontarf in 1014, was the first to use the name in true hereditary fashion.

Despite losing most of their possessions in the catastrophic seventeenth-century wars, the succession to the head of the sept continued unbroken to the present incumbent, Walter Lionel O'Kelly of Gallagh and Tycooly, Count of the Holy Roman Empire, known as 'The O'Kelly', and recognised as such by the Chief Herald of Ireland.

Kelly and O'Kelly are now almost as numerous as Murphy, and are found throughout Ireland. Individuals of the name have been prominent in all spheres of national life.

DEMOGRAPHIC DATA

TRADITIONAL FAMILY AREAS
Antrim, Derry, Down, Galway, Laois,
Meath, Roscommon, Sligo, Wicklow

FAMILY RANKING
1890: 2nd *1996*: 2nd

NO. OF BIRTHS
1890:1242

Famous Names

OISÍN KELLY (1915–1981)
Oisín Kelly was the best-known modern Irish sculptor.

CHARLES E. KELLY (1902–1981)
One of the founders of *Dublin Opinion*, the most famous satirical
magazine to appear in Ireland.

JAMES O'KELLY (1845–1916)
A man with a remarkable career: he served first as an officer in the French
Foreign Legion, then became a war correspondent, seeing action in Cuba,
Brazil and during the US Army's campaign against Sioux chief Sitting
Bull. In 1880 he was elected to Westminster as Member of Parliament for
Roscommon, and with one brief interruption, he held his seat until his
death in 1916.

Kennedy

HERALDIC BLAZON
Sable three helmets in
profile proper

Kennedy in Irish is Ó Cinneide, from a compound word meaning 'ugly-headed' or 'rough-headed'. The original bearer of the name, from whom the family claim descent, was a nephew of Brian Ború. His descendants were one of the most powerful families in the famous Dál gCais tribal grouping, and migrated from their homeland near Killaloe in Clare into adjoining north Tipperary, to become Lords of Ormond for over four hundred years up to the sixteenth century. As the family grew in numbers and power, it divided into three branches. known as Donn (brown), Fionn (fair) and Ruadh (red). From Tipperary the surname rapidly spread farther afield, becoming in the process one of the most numerous and widespread names in Ireland, to the point where it is now one of the twenty most common surnames in the country. No fewer than twenty-two placenames all over the country record the family's presence, including Ballykennedys in Antrim, Limerick and Waterford, Cappaghkennedy and Killokennedy in Clare, and in Wicklow, Newtownmountkennedy.

A branch of the southern Kennedys migrated to Co. Antrim at the start of the 17th century and many of the name in Ulster will be of this lineage. However, many Ulster Kennedys are originally of Scottish stock, the MacKennedys being a branch of the Clan Cameron. This family produced the Lords Kennedy, later Earls of Cassilis. The surname is now also very common in Galloway and Ayrshire in southwest Scotland.

Famous Names

JOHN F. KENNEDY (1917–1963) AND THE KENNEDY FAMILY

The most famous modern bearers of the name are, of course, John F. Kennedy, thirty-fifth president of the USA, and his brothers, Robert and Edward; they are descended from a Wexford branch of the Dalcassian family.

SIR ARTHUR KENNEDY (1810–1883)

A member of the Ulster family, had a long and successful career in the British colonial service, becoming in turn governor of Gambia, Hong Kong, Queensland and West Australia.

JIMMY KENNEDY (1902–1984)

Also of the Ulster Kennedys, Jimmy Kennedy was one of the most successful popular lyricists of the century, with such songs as *The Teddy Bears' Picnic*, *Red Sails in the Sunset* and *South of the Border* to his credit. He received an OBE in 1983.

SISTER STANISLAUS KENNEDY (b. 1939)

An outspoken campaigner for the poor and the homeless in Ireland.

Keogh

HERALDIC BLAZON
Argent a lion rampant gules, in the dexter chief a dexter hand couped at the wrist and in the sinister a crescent both of the second

Keogh and its variant, Kehoe, are the anglicisations of the Irish Mac hEochaidh, from *eoch*, meaning 'horse'. It arose as a surname in three distinct areas.

The first was in south Roscommon, around Moyfinn in the barony of Athlone, which used to be known as 'Keogh's country'. Keoghville in Taghmaconnell parish is named for them. This family was part of the Uí Maine tribal grouping, and were a branch of the O'Kellys.

The second was in west Tipperary, near Limerick city; the placename Ballymackeogh marks the centre of their territory. A branch of the family based at Castletroy in Limerick spelled the name K'eogh.

The third and most important both numerically and historically, was in Leinster, where the original homeland was in north Kildare, whence they migrated first to Wicklow, and then south to Wexford. Here they were hereditary poets to the O'Byrnes, with whom, tradition has it, they shared their ancestry. Their literary fame survived well into the moden period; Maolmuire MacKeogh is described in the *Annals of the Four Masters* as 'chief professor of poetry in Leinster'. A more recent practitioner was Padraig Kehoe of Enniscorthy (d.1959), prominent in the Gaelic Revivial and in the War of Independence, who wrote prolifically under the pen-name Hy Kinsella.

It is in Wexford that the name has been most commonly anglicised Kehoe. The surname is now most frequently found in Leinster, though it has become widespread throughout Ireland.

DEMOGRAPHIC DATA

TRADITIONAL FAMILY AREAS
Roscommon, Tipperary, Wexford

FAMILY RANKING
1890: 119th   *1996*: 82nd

NO. OF BIRTHS
1890: 163

Famous Names

WILLIAM KEOGH (1817–1878)

This member of the Keoghville family was an MP, a founder of the Catholic Defence Association and a campaigner for tenants' rights. Later, on becoming a judge, his opinions shifted, and the severity of his judgements in the trial of the Fenians in 1865 made him violently unpopular.

SIR ALFRED KEOGH (1857–1936)

Roscommon-born director-general of the British Army Medical Service before and during the First World War.

MYLES KEOGH (1848–1876)

A native of Carlow, who enjoyed an intense and varied military career. He fought first with the Papal forces in Italy, then on the Union side in the American Civil War, and finally with General Custer in the Indian wars. He died with Custer at the Battle of the Little Big Horn. Myles Keogh's horse, Commanche, was the only survivor on the US Army side.

The
Counties
of Ireland

DONEGAL
LONDONDERRY
ANTRIM
TYRONE
DOWN
LEITRIM
FERMANAGH
MONAGHAN
ARMAGH
SLIGO
MAYO
CAVAN
LOUTH
ROSCOMMON
LONGFORD
MEATH
WESTMEATH
DUBLIN
GALWAY
OFFALY
KILDARE
CLARE
LAOIS
WICKLOW
TIPPERARY
CARLOW
KILKENNY
LIMERICK
WEXFORD
KERRY
WATERFORD
CORK

AHERNE

BARRETT

BARRY

BOYLE

BRADY

BRENNAN

BURKE

BUTLER

BYRNE

CAHILL

CARROLL

CASEY

CASSIDY

CLANCY

CLEARY

CONNOLLY

COSTELLO

COUGHLAN

CROWLEY

CULLEN

DALY

DEMPSEY

DILLON

DOHERTY

DONNELLY

DONOVAN

DOWD

DOWLING

DOYLE

DUGGAN

DUNNE

DWYER

EGAN

FAHY

FARRELL

FINNEGAN

FITZGERALD

FLAHERTY

FLANAGAN

FLEMING

FLYNN

GALLACHER

HENNESSY

HICKEY

HIGGINS

HOGAN

JOYCE

KAVANAGH

KEANE

KEARNEY

KEATING

KEOGH

KELLY

KENNEDY

LYNCH

MACAULEY

McCANN

MACARTHY

MACDERMOT

MACDONAGH

MACDONNELL

MACEVOY

MACGOVERN

MACGRATH

MACGUINNESS

MACHUGH

MACKENNA

MACKEON

MACLOUGHLIN

MACMAHON

MACMANUS

MACNALLY

MACNAMARA

MACSWEENY

MADDEN

MAGUIRE

MAHER

MALONE

MARTIN

MEEHAN

MOLLOY

MOLONEY

MONAGHAN

MOONEY

MORAN

MORIARTY

MORRIS

MULLAN

MURPHY

NOLAN

O'BRIEN

O'CALLAGHAN

O'CONNELL

O'CONNOR

O'DONNELL

O'DONOGHUE

O'DRISCOLL

O'HARA

O'KEEFE

O'LEARY

O'MAHONY

O'NEILL

O'REILLY

O'RIORDAN

O'SHEA

O'SULLIVAN

O'TOOLE

POWER

QUIGLEY

QUINN

REDMOND

REGAN

ROCHE

ROURKE

RYAN

SHEEHAN

SHERIDAN

TOBIN

WALSH

WHELAN

ULSTER

CONNAUGHT

LEINSTER

MUNSTER

The
Provinces
of Ireland

Lynch

HERALDIC BLAZON
Azure a chevron between
three trefoils slipt or

Lynch, which is today one of the most common surnames in Ireland, is unusual in that it has two completely distinct origins. The first is Norman, from de Lench, possibly derived from a French placename now forgotten. The family settled initially in Co. Meath, then a branch established itself in Galway where they rapidly became one of the strongest of the famous Tribes of Galway; between 1484 and 1654, no fewer than eighty-four city mayors were Lynches. One of these, James Lynch, mayor in 1493, is reputed to have hanged his own son for murder when no-one else would carry out the sentence. The arms illustrated, a classic example of the simplicity of Norman heraldry, are for this family. In Ireland, the term 'lynching' is believed to be derived from this James Lynch, although in the USA the likeliest origin is usually cited as the eighteenth-century American justice of the peace, Charles Lynch, who ordered extralegal punishment for criminal acts during the American War of Independence.

The name's second origin is Gaelic, from the Irish Ó Loingsigh, or grandson of Loingseach, meaning 'seaman'. Given the importance of the sea in Irish life, the surname naturally arose quite separately in many areas, including Clare/Limerick, Sligo, west Cork, Cavan, Donegal and north Antrim/Derry. In west Cork, the family were initially among the leaders of the Tuath Ó nDunghalaigh, based near modern Clonakilty, and are recorded in the sixteenth and seventeenth centuries as chiefs of an area in the Beara peninsula, in the parish of Kilcaskan, under O'Sullivan Beare's overlordship. They were finally dispossessed in the late seventeenth century.

Famous Names

JOHN MARY ('JACK') LYNCH (b. 1917)

Taoiseach from 1966 to 1973 and from 1977 to 1979, Jack Lynch is undoubtedly the best-known contemporary Lynch in Ireland. He himself was born in Cork city, though his family originated in west Cork. He was, surprisingly, the first Corkman to become Taoiseach.

DAVID LYNCH

Outside Ireland the name has also become well-known; David Lynch has directed some of the strangest and most intriguing films of recent years, such as *Eraserhead* and *Blue Velvet*, as well as the classic television series *Twin Peaks*.

Better known on Wall Street would be one of the largest US investment banks, Merrill Lynch.

MacAuley

HERALDIC BLAZON
Argent a lion rampant gules
armed and langued azure in
chief two dexter hands couped
at the wrist of the second

MacAuley and its many variants – Cawley, Gawley, Macauley, Magawley, etc. – may be either Scottish or Irish in origin. They are anglicisations of two distinct Irish surnames, Mac Amhalgaidh ('son of Auley') and Mac Amhlaoibh ('son of Auliff'). The former derives from a native personal name now obsolete, and the family of that surname ruled a territory in what is now Offaly/Westmeath. The centre of their power was near Ballyloughnoe in Co. Westmeath, at the heart of what the English called 'McGawley's country'.

In Ulster, the name derives from Mac Amhlaoibh, incorporating a Gaelic version of the common Norse name Olaf. The family claim descent from Amhlaoibh, son of Donn Carrach Maguire, the first Maguire king of Fermanagh who ruled at the end of the thirteenth century. The family are reputed to have conquered south Fermanagh for the Maguires. They gave their name to the barony of Clanawley in that county. Mac Amhlaoibh is also the Irish original of an entirely distinct family, the MacAuliffs of Munster, who are descended from Amhlaoibh MacCarthy.

In Scotland also the surname and its variants, coincidentally, have the same two distinct origins – Gaelic and Norse personal names. The MacAulays of Lewis share their ancestry with the MacLeods. The MacAulays of Dunbartonshire are a secondary branch of the Clan Alpin. The Scots origin is most common in northeast Ulster, where a branch of the MacAuleys settled in the sixteenth century.

In 1890 MacAuley was most numerous in Antrim and Donegal, with Gawley found in Sligo and Cawley in both Mayo and Sligo.

DEMOGRAPHIC DATA

TRADITIONAL FAMILY AREAS
Fermanagh, Offaly, Westmeath

FAMILY RANKING
1890: 210th   *1996*: 223rd

NO. OF BIRTHS
1890: 107

Famous Names

CATHERINE MCAULEY (1787–1841)

Founder of the Mercy Order of nuns, now active world-wide. She is depicted on the Irish £5 note.

DAVE MCAULEY (b. 1961)

This member of the Antrim McAuleys was a well-known boxer. He became British flyweight champion in 1986 and IBF world champion in 1989. He defended the title successfully five times, before losing it in 1992 on a points decision which still arouses controversy today.

McCann

HERALDIC BLAZON
Azure fretty or, on a
fess argent a boar
passant gules

There is dispute as to whether McCann comes from the Irish Mac Anna, 'son of Annadh', or Mac Cana, from *cana*, meaning 'wolf cub'. At any rate, the major family of the name were known as lords of Clanbrassil, an area on the southern shores of Lough Neagh in the modern Co. Armagh, which they conquered from the O'Garveys. They appear to have been a branch of the Cenél Eoghain, the large group of families claiming descent from Eoghan, one of the sons of Niall of the Nine Hostages, the fifth century founder of the Uí Néill dynasty. The death in 1155 of one of their chiefs, Amhlaoibh Mac Cana, is recorded in the *Annals of the Four Masters* with praise for his chivalry, his vigour, and the fine strong drink he made from the apples in his orchard. Armagh apples are still renowned for their flavour. The last recorded Chief of the Name, Donall MacCanna, was still known as lord of Clanbrassil as late as 1598.

Today, the surname is found principally in counties Armagh, Tyrone and Antrim, though it has also spread southwards into the provinces of Leinster and Connacht.

The family name is recorded in the townland of Annagh McCann's in Louth parish in Co. Louth.

DEMOGRAPHIC DATA

TRADITIONAL FAMILY AREAS
Armagh

FAMILY RANKING
1890: 102nd   *1996*: 70th

NO. OF BIRTHS
1890: 177

Famous Names

PATRICK MCCANNA

A member of the United Irishmen in Paris during the post-Revolutionary period known as the Terror. He accompanied Wolfe Tone on his expedition to Ireland and went on to become successful merchant in Boulogne.

TOMÁS MAC ANNA (b. 1920)

Artistic director of the Abbey Theatre for many years.

FERDIA MAC ANNA

Tomás Mac Anna's son Ferdia is well-known as a novelist, particularly for *The Last of the High Kings* (1992), despite an earlier incarnation as Rocky De Valera, leader of the proto-punk Rocky De Valera and the Gravediggers.

JOHN MCCANN (1905–1980)

An extremely popular playwright in his day, as well a successful politician.

DONAL MCCANN (b. 1943)

The son of John McCann, Donal has had international success as a stage and film actor.

MacCarthy

HERALDIC BLAZON
Argent a stag trippant
gules attired and
unguled or

MacCarthy comes from the Irish Mac Carthaigh, from *carthach*, 'loving'. The original Carthach from whom the surname is taken was king of Cashel c. 1040, when Donncha, son of Brian Ború, was king of Munster. Carthach was part of the dynasty claiming descent from Eoghan, one of the sons of Oiloll Ollum, the semi-legendary third-century king of Munster. The Eoghanacht, as they were known, had dominated Munster virtually unchallenged until the meteoric rise of Brian, part of the rival Dál gCais, who claimed descent from another son of Oiloll Ollum, Cas. The Eoghanacht resisted the Dál gCais fiercely, with the result that the MacCarthys and the O'Briens, with their respective allies, waged bitter, intermittent war for almost a century and a half. In the mid twelfth century the struggle ended with the MacCarthys' expulsion from their homeland in the Golden Vale in Co. Tipperary. They moved south, into the historic territory of Desmond, and it is with this area, which includes modern counties Cork and Kerry, that they have been strongly associated ever since.

Nevertheless, the family retained their ability to rule, dominating much of Munster for almost five centuries. There were four distinct branches: those led by the MacCarthy Mór ('Great MacCarthy'), nominal head of all the MacCarthys, who ruled over much of south Kerry; the Duhallow MacCarthys, controlling northwest Cork; MacCarthy Riabhach ('grey') based in Carbery in southwest Cork; and MacCarthy Muskerry, on the Cork/Kerry border. Each continued to offer resistance to Norman and English encroachments up to the seventeenth century when they finally succumbed.

DEMOGRAPHIC DATA

TRADITIONAL FAMILY AREAS
Cork, Kerry

FAMILY RANKING
1890: 11th *1996*: 13th

NO. OF BIRTHS
1890: 498

Famous Names

JUSTIN MACCARTHY (d. 1694)

After the great scattering of the Gaelic aristocracy at the end of the seventeenth century the MacCarthys, like so many others, became prominent in the armies of the Catholic kings of Europe. Justin MacCarthy, the first Duc de Clancarthy, was the founder of the Irish Brigade in the army of Louis XlV of France. The last in the line, Pol MacCarthy, was the 7th Duc and fought in the army of Napoleon III.

EUGENE MCCARTHY

Eugene McCarthy was US senator for Minnesota from 1958 to 1970, and a one-time Democratic party candidate for the presidency.

SENATOR JOSEPH MCCARTHY (1909–1957)

His less salubrious namesake made his reputation through a ferocious anti-Communist witch-hunt and left the term McCarthyism in the political lexicon.

MacDermot

HERALDIC BLAZON
Argent on a chevron gules
between three boars heads
erased azure tusked and
bristled or as many cross
crosslets of the last

The surname MacDermot (and its variants MacDermott, McDermot, etc.) comes from the Irish Mac Dhiarmada, 'son of Dermot'. The meaning of the personal name Diarmuid, on which the surname is based, remains uncertain. Two separate derivations have been argued, one from *dia*, meaning 'god' and *armaid* 'of arms', the other from d*í-fhormaid*, 'unenvious'. The individual from whom the surname is taken lived in the twelfth century, and was himself a direct descendant of Maelruanaidh Mór, brother of Conor, King of Connacht, the ancestor of the O'Connors, who ruled in the tenth century. Tradition has it that the two brothers agreed that in return for surrendering claim to the kingship of Connacht, Maelruanaidh and his descendants would receive the territory of Moylurg, an area in northern modern Co. Roscommon which includes the modern towns of Boyle and Frenchpark. Certainly this is the area with which Maelruanaidh's descendants, the MacDermots, have been closely associated down to modern times. For centuries their seat was a large castle on MacDermot's Island, in Lough Key just outside Boyle.

The Moylurg branch remained powerful in their homeland until the final post-Cromwellian confiscations, when they were lost their lands. But unlike others who suffered similarly, the MacDermots of Moylurg managed to salvage some of their possessions. In the seventeenth century they moved to Coolavin, beside Lough Gara in Co. Sligo, where the line of descent from the original MacDermot chiefs remains unbroken. The current head of the family, known as The MacDermot, Prince of Coolavin, is Niall Mac Dermot.

Famous Names

HUGH MACDERMOT (1834–1904)

Head of the Moylurg family, he was was Solicitor General and Attorney-General for Ireland.

FRANK MACDERMOT (1886–1975)

Hugh MacDermot's son, who was a barrister and politician in his early life. But disillusionment with life and politics in De Valera's Ireland drove him to emigrate to the US and, later, to France, where he became well-known as a journalist and author.

MacDonagh

MacDonagh, and its many variants, MacDonough, Donogh, Donaghy, etc., all derive from the Irish Mac Donnchadha, from Donnchadh (often anglicised as Donagh), a popular first name meaning 'brown one'. The early popularity of the name meant that the surname based on it arose separately in a number of places. In Co. Cork, where the MacDonaghs were known as Lords of Duhallow and had their seat at Kanturk, the family were a branch of the MacCarthys. The name is now rare in Cork.

In Connacht another family arose, a branch of the MacDermotts, claiming Donagh MacDermott as their ancestor. Their power was concentrated in counties Roscommon and Sligo, where the family were rulers in the barony of Tirreril. It is thought that a separate Connacht family, based in Co. Galway, were part of the O'Flahertys. In Ulster, a variant of Mac Donnchadha was Mac Donnchaidh, common in Derry and Tyrone, and also anglicised as MacDonaghy and Donaghy. However, as is so often the case in Ulster, there is also a Scottish family, the Clan Donachie, part of the Clan Robertson, with an identically anglicised surname. Without detailed genealogical investigation it can be very difficult to tell which of the two origins applies.

Today Donaghy is almost exclusively found in Ulster, particularly in Antrim and Tyrone, while MacDonagh is overwhelmingly a Connacht name, concentrated in Galway, Mayo and Roscommon.

DEMOGRAPHIC DATA

TRADITIONAL FAMILY AREAS
Sligo, Roscommon

FAMILY RANKING
1890: 107th *1996*: 152nd

NO. OF BIRTHS
1890: 174

Famous Names

THOMAS MACDONAGH (1878–1916)

A distinguished poet and a lecturer in University College Dublin who edited the *Irish Review* and, with Edward Martyn, helped to found the Irish Theatre. He is best remembered for his part in the 1916 rising. He was one of the 'signatories' of the Proclamation of Independence and was executed after the rising.

DONAGH MACDONAGH (1912–68)

Thomas MacDonagh's son was a poet, dramatist and lawyer, whose most successful play, *Happy as Larry*, has been translated into a dozen languages.

THE MACDONAGH SISTERS

The MacDonagh Sisters were early stars of the Australian cinema. *The Far Paradise* (1928) is an enduring classic.

MacDonnell

HERALDIC BLAZON
Azure an ancient galley sails set and flags flying argent between in chief a cross cavalry in three grieces or, between in the dexter an increscent of the second and in the sinister a dexter hand couped at the apaumée proper and in base a salmon naiant of the second

MacDonnell comes from the Irish Mac Domhnaill, from the personal name Domhnall, a compound of 'world' and 'strong'. Widely distributed throughout Ireland, the principal source of the name is Scottish. Grandsons of Donald of Islay came to Ulster in the fourteenth century as mercenaries for the Irish chiefs and rapidly acquired territory and power there – in Tyrone, Fermanagh, Monaghan and Antrim – and elsewhere. The Burkes are reputed to have first brought them to Mayo. Somhairle Buidhe ('Sorley Boy') MacDonnell conquered a large part of Co. Antrim in the sixteenth century and defended it tenaciously against Gaelic Irish and English intrusions. In 1620 his son, Randal MacSorley MacDonnell, was created Earl of Antrim. Given the origin of the surname, the confusion with MacDonald is understandable; Irish MacDonalds, in fact, share their ancestry with most Irish McDonnells. Also, the Antrim pronunciation of the original Irish has sometimes led to the anglicisation MacConnell or Connell.

Problematically, there are also several native Irish sources for the surname. In Ulster, the most prominent native family were the MacDonnells of Clankelly, rulers of Fermanagh before the rise of the Maguires. Displaced on losing power, they settled in the north of Co. Monaghan, and remain numerous in the area. Another family arose in the old kingdom of Thomond, in the Clare/Limerick area, where the MacDonnells were hereditary poets to the O'Briens.

DEMOGRAPHIC DATA

TRADITIONAL FAMILY AREAS
Antrim, Fermanagh, Mayo,
Monaghan, Tyrone

FAMILY RANKING
1890: 61st *1996*: 76th

NO. OF BIRTHS
1890: 247

Famous Names

SEÁN CLÁRACH MACDONNELL (1691–1754)
The most famous poet in Munster in his day.

ALEXANDER MACDONNELL (1798–1835)
A Belfast native who was one of the greatest chess players of his day. He
was world chess champion in 1833.

SIR ANTONY MACDONNELL (1844–1925)
This member of the Mayo family had a distinguished career in the British
civil service, becoming Lieutenant-Governor of Agra and Oudh in 1895.
From 1902 to 1908 he headed the Irish civil service and played a large
part in the reforms of his day, including the transfers of land ownership
to small tenants. He became Baron MacDonnell of Swineford in 1908.

MacEvoy

HERALDIC BLAZON

Per fess azure and per pale or
and ermine a fess gules issuant
therefrom a demi-lion argent,
in the dexter base a dexterhand
couped at the wrist of the
fourth

MacEvoy (or MacAvoy) is the phonetic anglicisation of Mac Fhiodhbhuidhe, possibly from the Irish *fiodhbhadhach*, 'man of the woods'. The most prominent family of the name originally held power in the barony of Moygoish in modern Co. Westmeath, but migrated southwest, where they became one of the well-known Seven Septs of Leix, ruling over an area in the parishes of Mountrath and Raheen in Co. Laois.

In the early seventeenth century, the most important leaders of the family were forcibly transported to Co. Kerry, together with other members of the Seven Septs, but the surname remains numerous in the Laois/Westmeath region. In the north of the country, MacEvoy was used as an erroneous equivalent of Mac Giolla Bhuidhe, 'son of the fair-haired youth', a Donegal name usually anglicised as McIlwee or MacKelvey, and of Mac an Bheatha, 'son of life' (MacVeigh), a surname common in the Armagh/Louth region.

In 1890 the surname was recorded as most common in the Armagh/Louth area.

Famous Names

FRANCIS MacEVOY (1751–1804)

A one-time president of the Royal College of Surgeons of Ireland.

ELEANOR McEVOY (b. 1967)

One of a group of extremely successful women singer–songwriters to emerge in Ireland in the early 1990s. She began her career as a violinist in the National Symphony Orchestra, but went solo in 1991 after the release of her first record. She has won numerous awards.

MacGovern

HERALDIC BLAZON

Azure a lion passant or,
in chief three crescents
of the last

MacGovern is the phonetic anglicisation of Mag Shamhradhain, from a diminutive of *samradh*, 'summer'; it has also occasionally been anglicised as Summers or Somers. The name is closely linked with the original homeland where it first arose; in the traditional genealogies, Samhradhan, the eleventh-century gentleman from whom the surname comes, was himself descended from Eochadh, one of the O'Rourkes, who lived in the eighth century. His name was given to the area of Co. Cavan where the MacGoverns held sway, the barony of Tullyhaw (Teallach Eochaidh) in the northwest of the county. The particular centres of their power were Bawnaboy, Lissanover, and Ballymagauran. This last includes an earlier anglicisation of Mag Shamhradhain, Magauran or MacGowran, now much less common than MacGovern. In the old kingdom of Breffny, the family were highly influential, contributing many clerics to the church. *The Book of the Magaurans* is a well-known fourteenth century manuscript of poems, chiefly concerning the family itself.

From Cavan the name has now spread throughout Connacht and Ulster, and is particularly numerous in the adjoining counties of Fermanagh and Leitrim. Magauran/McGowran is virtually exclusive to Cavan.

DEMOGRAPHIC DATA

TRADITIONAL FAMILY AREAS
Cavan, Fermanagh, Leitrim

FAMILY RANKING
1890: 222nd *1996*: 231st

NO. OF BIRTHS
1890: 102

Famous Names

JACK MACGOWRAN (1918–1973)

One of Ireland's best actors, renowned for his interpretations of the works of Samuel Beckett. In 1971 he became the first non-American ever to received the New York Critics' Actor of the Year Award.

GEORGE STANLEY MCGOVERN (b. 1922)

This well-known American political leader was the Democratic presidential nominee in 1972 and represented South Dakota in both the US House of Representatives (1956–1960) and the Senate (1962–1980).

EILIS MCGOVERN (b. 1955)

The first woman member of the council of the Royal College of Surgeons of Ireland, and one of Ireland's leading heart surgeons.

MacGrath

HERALDIC BLAZON

Quarterly: 1st, Argent three lions passant gules; 2nd, Or a dexter hand lying fessways couped at the wrist proper holding a cross formée fitchée azure; 3rd, Gules a dexter hand lying fessways couped at the wrist proper holding a battle-axe r; 4th, Argent an antelope trippant sable attired or.

MacGrath, and its many variants – Magrath, MacGraw, Magra, Magraw – comes from the Irish Mac Raith, from the personal name Rath, meaning 'grace' or 'prosperity'.

Two native Irish families adopted the name. The first was based on the borders of the modern counties of Donegal and Fermanagh, around Termon MacGrath, and were *erenaghs* (hereditary abbots) of the monastery of St Daveoc on Lough Derg. Castle Magrath, dating from the sixteenth century, stands in Pettigo in Co. Fermanagh. The most remarkable bearer of the name was of this family, Meiler Magrath (1523–1622), who managed to be, simultaneously, Catholic Bishop of Down and Connor and Protestant Archbishop of Cashel. His rapacity was notorious, and he held six Anglican bishoprics, four of them at the one time, as well as the income of seventy parishes

The other family were originally based in Co. Clare, where they were famous as hereditary poets and genealogists to the ruling O'Brien family of Thomond. One of this family John Mac Cratih wrote the eleventh-century history *The Wars of Turlough*.

Today neither area has large numbers of the surname. The southern family spread eastwards into counties Tipperary and Waterford, while the northern family's descendants are now mainly to be found in Co. Tyrone, where they settled around Ardstraw. Descendants of the Clare family were responsible for the famous bardic school at Cahir.

DEMOGRAPHIC DATA

TRADITIONAL FAMILY AREAS
Clare, Donegal, Fermanagh

FAMILY RANKING
1890: 51st *1996*: 45th

NO. OF BIRTHS
1890: 266

Famous Names

JOSEPH MCGRATH (1877–1966)

Joseph McGrath was involved in the 1916 rising and became Minister for Labour and subsequently Minister for Industry and Commerce in the new Irish government. He went on to a successful business career, founding a dynasty which continues to the present.

SIR PATRICK THOMAS MAGRATH (1868–1929)

A descendent from the Waterford family. He became President of the Upper House of the Newfoundland legislature in Canada.

ANDREW CONDON MAGRATH (1813–1893)

Son of refugee from the 1798 rebellion who fought on the Confederate side in the American Civil War, and went on to become Governor of South Carolina.

JAMES MAGRATH (1835–1898)

This member of the Tipperary family was an Oblate Missionary, and became the first Provincial of the Oblate Fathers in the US.

MacGuinness

HERALDIC BLAZON

Vert a lion rampant or, on
a chief argent a dexter
hand erect couped at
the wrist gules

MacGuinness, with its variants Guinness, Magennis, MacNeice, MacCreesh, etc., comes from the Irish Mac Aonghusa, from the personal name Aonghus (Angus), made up of *aon*, 'one', and *ghus*, 'choice'; it was borne by an eighth-century Pictish king in Scotland, said to be a son of the Irish god Daghda and Boann, the goddess after whom the Boyne is named. The surname originated in Iveagh, in what is now Co. Down; legend has it Iveagh (Uí Eachaigh) took its name from Eocha Cobha, a semi-mythical ancestor of Aonghus.

The MacGuinnesses displaced the O'Haugheys in the twelfth century, ruling virtually all of Co. Down for four centuries. Like others of the Gaelic aristocracy, they had an elaborate and strongly pre-Christian inauguration for their leader, the chief of their name. It centred on the Coiseach Aonghuis, Aongus's footstone, with the imprint of a foot in the rock; if a true MacGuinness placed his foot in it, a 'pleasant humming sound' would result. Needless to say, impostors, and their fraudulent feet, met unspeakable ends. The stone is still exists outside Warrenpoint in Co. Down.

Their centre of power was at Rathfriland, ten miles from Newry. In the sixteenth century they accepted the Reformation, but joined in the later wars against the English. They were dispossessed and the castle at Rathfriland was destroyed in 1641. The name is now common in Connacht and Leinster, as well as its original Ulster homeland.

Variants of the name include MacCreesh, found in Monaghan, Fermanagh and south Down, and MacNiece or MacNeice, found in Antrim.

DEMOGRAPHIC DATA

TRADITIONAL FAMILY AREAS
Armagh, Down

FAMILY RANKING
1890: 169th   *1996*: 172th

NO. OF BIRTHS
1890: 128

Famous Names

ARTHUR GUINNESS AND THE GUINNESS FAMILY

The most famous instance of the surname is, of course, in the name of the black beer brewed at St James's Gate in Dublin. The founder of the brewery, Arthur Guinness, came from a family long settled in Celbridge in Co. Kildare, but with roots in Co. Down. Although Guinness is now a multi-national company, the descendants of the founder are still prominent in its management. The family awareness of the antiquity of its ancestral connections is reflected in the choice of title when Edward Cecil Guinness was created First Earl of Iveagh in 1909. This was, in fact, the second creation. The first Viscounts Iveagh were supporters of King James in the Williamite wars; after his defeat Brian Magennis, second Viscount Iveagh, fought and died with the Austrian Imperial Army as the head of Iveagh's regiment, while his brother Roger, third Viscount Iveagh, fought in the armies of both France and Spain.

LOUIS MACNEICE (1907–1963)

Belfast-born and English-educated poet. In the 1930s he was associated with the group of young poets which included Auden, Spencer and Day-Lewis. The better-known Northern Irish poets of the 1970s and '80s have claimed his mordant, witty and well-crafted poems as poetic forebears.

MacHugh

HERALDIC BLAZON
Argent a saltire vert between a dexter hand couped at the wrist gules, two trefoils slipt of the second in fess and a boat with oars proper in base

Along with its principal variant, MacCue, MacHugh comes from the Irish Mac Aodha or Aoidhe, from the very popular personal name Aodh, meaning 'fire'. In various forms, Aodh is the root of a large number of common surnames, Eason, Hayes, McCoy, Hughes and Magee among them.

At least two distinct families in west Ulster and Connacht adopted Mac Aodha: a branch of the O'Flahertys of Connemara based near the modern town of Tuam in north Galway, in what was then the barony of Clare and, in Fermanagh, a family who claim descent from Aodh, a grandson of Donn Carrach Maguire, the first Maguire ruler of the county. Many of the Fermanagh family have changed to Magee or McGee, which approximates more closely to the Fermanagh pronunciation. Today the surname is most numerous in Co. Donegal and in north Connacht, though it is also common in Leinster.

The surname's dramatic slippage in the numerical rankings between 1890 and 1996 is presumably because of reversions and changes such as that which has happened in Fermanagh.

DEMOGRAPHIC DATA

TRADITIONAL FAMILY AREAS
Fermanagh, Galway

FAMILY RANKING
1890: 103rd *1996*: 140th

BIRTHS
1890: 176

Famous Names

MALACHY MACHUGH

Malachy MacHugh, of the Galway family, was a celebrated bishop of
Elphin and Archbishop of Tuam in the early fourteenth century.

ROGER MACHUGH (1908–1987)

A well-known critic, playwright and academic who was professor of
English at University College Dublin from 1965 to 1967 and professor of
Anglo-Irish Literature from 1967 to 1978. He is remembered for his
studies of Anglo-Irish literature, particularly his *Short History of Anglo-
Irish Literature* (1982).

MacKenna

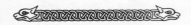

HERALDIC BLAZON
Vert a fess argent
between three lions'
heads affrontée or

MacKenna is the English form of the Irish surname Mac Cionaoith. The Mac Cionaoith were originally based in Meath, but in early times were brought north into Clogher as hired fighters by the rulers of that territory, and quickly became lords in their own right controlling Truagh, a territory on the borders of the modern counties of Tyrone and Monaghan. Their power endured down to the seventeenth century, their last chief being Patrick McKenna, who died near Emyvale Co. Monaghan in 1616. Another branch of this family settled in Co. Down in the seventeenth century, near the town of Maghera.

The name is one of the few for which anglicisation, the loss of the 'Mac' prefix, has never worked. The surname is still very numerous in the area of the original homeland, to the point where suffixes and local nicknames are necessary to identify the different families of the name. Over the centuries, however, it has spread throughout the country.

In the century since Matheson's survey of the frequency of Irish surnames, the McKennas appear to have gone forth and multiplied. Ranked 89th in 1890, by 1996 they were at 68th in the Republic of Ireland and 52nd in Northern Ireland, based on telephone directory listings.

TRADITIONAL FAMILY AREAS
Monaghan, Tyrone

FAMILY RANKING
1890: 89th   *1996*: 68th

NO. OF BIRTHS
1890: 201

Famous Names

JUAN MACKENNA (1771–1814)

Born at Clogher in Co. Tyrone, he was educated in Barcelona and became governor of Oserno in Chile. He became a general under the Liberator Bernardo O'Higgins in the fight for Chilean independence and was killed in a duel with one of O'Higgins' opponents.

SIOBHÁN MCKENNA (1921–86)

The most famous Irish actress of her generation, she was renowned for her parts in Shaw's *St Joan* and Murphy's *Bailegangaire*.

T. P. MCKENNA (b. 1929)

Originally from Cavan, T. P. McKenna is well-known on television, in films and on the stage of Dublin's Abbey Theatre.

MARTIN MCKENNA (1832–1907)

An emigrant to Australia in 1845 where he set up the Campaspe Brewery. He also became a respected politician and farmer.

MacKeon

MacKeon has a wide range of synonyms and variants, including Keon, MacKeown, MacEoin, MacGeown, MacOwen, and in Ulster, MacEwan, MacCune, MacKone, Magowen and, occasionally, Johnson or Johnstone. The reason lies in the Irish and Scottish original of the name, Mac Eoghain, 'son of Eoin (John)', which arose independently in a number of areas. In Ireland the principal areas of origin were in the Kiltartan region of Co. Galway, at Creggan and Derrynoone in Co. Armagh and in Sligo/Leitrim in north Connacht. This last family were the most prominent historically, and it is thought that the Galway family were an offshoot. In Co. Antrim, the surname is almost entirely of Scottish origin, and derives from Eoin Bissett, who came to the Glens of Antrim from Scotland in the thirteenth century. The form MacKeown is largely confined to northeast Ulster, while MacKeon is most common in Connacht and west Ulster. As so often with variations in spelling, however, no absolute rules are possible.

In addition, in Ulster especially, MacKeon may also be an Irish variant of the Scottish MacCune or MacCunn, itself based on MacEoghain. The name is well known in Galloway, the origin of many of those who came to Ulster in the seventeenth century, so it is probable that many MacKeo(w)ns in the North will be of this origin.

DEMOGRAPHIC DATA

TRADITIONAL FAMILY AREAS
Antrim, Armagh, Leitrim,
Galway, Sligo

FAMILY RANKING
1890: 105th   *1996*: 107th

NO. OF BIRTHS
1890: 175

Famous Names

MILES KEON

There have been two famous Miles Keons, one a successful nineteenth-century novelist, other an eighteenth-century political figure, both from Leitrim.

SEÁN MACEOIN

Seán MacEoin, from Ballinaee in Co. Longford and known as 'the blacksmith of Ballinalee', was prominent in the War of Independence and afterwards on the Pro-Treaty side in the Civil War. He was a minister in several post-independence governments and stood unsuccessfully against De Valera for the presidency in 1959.

SEÁN MACEOIN (b. 1910)

His namesake from Cooley in Co. Louth was Chief of Staff of the Irish Army from 1960 to 1971. Internationally he is best known for his command of the United Nations forces in the Congo in the early 1960s.

MacLoughlin

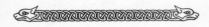

HERALDIC BLAZON

Per fess azure and gules, in chief a lion rampant or between two swords erect argent pommels and hilts or, in base three crescents argent

MacLoughlin is the form of the name most frequent in Connacht and Leinster, while McLaughlin is most common in Ulster, particularly in counties Antrim, Donegal and Derry. Both derive from the Irish and Scots Mac Lochlainn, from the personal name Lochlann, from *loch*, 'lake', and *lann*, 'land'. It was a Gaelic name used for Scandinavia, and was applied to the Viking settlers of the early Middle Ages, becoming a popular name in its own right. The surname containing it has at least four origins in Ireland.

In Connacht there were at least two families of the name, minor branches of the O'Connors and the MacDermotts. In the Inishowen peninsula of Co. Donegal, the family were among the northern Uí Néill , reputed descendants of the semi-mythical Niall of the Nine Hostages. They were the most powerful family of Cenél Eoghain, the tribal grouping claiming descent from Eogan, son of Niall, supplying eleven kings of that grouping and two High Kings between 1061 and 1241, when they were defeated by Brian Ó Néill, leader of their rivals in the Cenél Eoghain, whose family replaced them as rulers of Ulster. Although the family then fade from history, the nineteenth-century antiquarian John O'Donovan visited the reputed grave of Eogan, the progenitor of the Cenél Eoghain, in Iskaheen in the Inishowen peninsula in 1835 and reported meeting there 'MacLoughlin, Chief of his name'. MacLachlan and its variants is also common in Scotland; the Clan MacLachlan had their principal seat at Cowal in Argyll, and no doubt many McLaughlins in Ulster are of this stock.

DEMOGRAPHIC DATA

TRADITIONAL FAMILY AREAS
Donegal, Meath, Sligo, Roscommon

FAMILY RANKING
1890:21st *1996*: 53rd

NO. OF BIRTHS
1890: 391

Famous Names

JOHN MACLOUGHLIN (1784–1857)

A well-known character for his role in the history of the Hudson Bay company.

PEDRO MACLOCLIN (1791–1845)

The son of a Leitrim emigrant who became a successful merchant in Santiago, Chile, Pedro Macloclin gained fame in his father's adopted country for his work in astronomy.

ALF MAC LOCHLAIN (b. 1924)

The former director of the National Library of Ireland who is best known now for his humourous, semi-surreal fiction.

MacMahon

HERALDIC BLAZON

Argent three lions passant
reguardant in pale gules
armed and langued azure

MacMahon (or McMahon) comes from Mac Mathghamha or, in the modern version Mac Mathuna, from *mathghamhain*, 'bear'. The surname arose separately in two areas, in west Clare and in Co. Monaghan. In the former, the MacMahons were part of the Dál gCais tribal grouping, and claim decent from Mahon O'Brien, grandson of Brian Ború. The last Chief of the Name was killed at the Battle of Kinsale in 1602. The Ulster MacMahons were based in the barony of Truagh in the north of Monaghan, and ruled the kingdom of Oriel between the thirteenth and the sixteenth centuries. Their last chief, Hugh MacMahon, who had become a lieutenant-colonel in the Spanish army, was beheaded by the English in 1641.

A separate McMahon family in Fermanagh are descended from Mahon Maguire, a grandson of Donn Carrach Maguire. Today, although widespread throughout Ireland, MacMahon remains most common in the two ancestral homelands of Clare and Monaghan.

The name's anglicisation, to 'Mahon', was never extensive; in 1890 less than 25% recorded their names thus., and fewer still do today.

After the defeats of the native Irish in the seventeenth century, many Clare MacMahons emigrated to serve in the Irish Brigade of the French army. John Baptiste MacMahon, son of one of the original members of the Irish Brigade was made Marquis d'Eguilly by Louis XV. His grandson, Edmonde Patrice MacMahon (1808–93) was created Duke of Magenta, became a Field Marshal and President of France. The MacMahon family are still prominent in France; the family home is the Château de Sully outside Bordeaux.

DEMOGRAPHIC DATA

TRADITIONAL FAMILY AREAS
Clare, Fermanagh, Monaghan

FAMILY RANKING
1890: 66th   *1996*: 58th

NO. OF BIRTHS
1890: 241

Famous Names

BERNARD MACMAHON (d.1816)

An emigrant to Philadelphia in the USA who became an eminent botanist. His name is recorded in the evergreen shrub *berbeeris mahonia*.

CHARLES PATRICK MAHON (1800–91)

Known as 'The O'Gorman Mahon', he was a member of the Clare family. He was famous as an international soldier – Chile, Brazil, France and Russia are only some of the countries he served – and later as a politician in Parnell's Irish Party.

SIR CHARLES MACMAHON (1824–91)

A descendant of the Clare family who emigrated to Australia in 1853, became Commissioner of Police in Melbourne and secured election to the Legislative Assembly.

SIR WILLIAM MACMAHON (b. 1908)

Another prominent Australian MacMahon, who was Prime Minister of Australia in 1971 and 1972.

BRYAN MACMAHON (b. 1909)

One of Ireland's best-loved playwrights and short-story writers for almost sixty years.

MacManus

HERALDIC BLAZON
Vert a griffin sergeant
or in chief three
crescents argentf

MacManus is the anglicisation of the Irish Mac Maghnuis, from the popular Norse personal name Magnus, from the Latin *magnus*, 'great'. Although the Viking settlers are responsible for the introduction of Magnus as a personal name, the surname it gave rise to is entirely Irish. It came into being in two distinct areas: in Co. Roscommon, where the family claim descent from Maghnuis, son of the twelfth-century High King, Turlough O'Connor; and in Co. Fermanagh, where the original ancestor was Maghnuis Maguire, son of the chieftain Donn Mor Maguire. In Fermanagh they were second in power only to the Maguires themselves and, from their base on the island of Ballymaguire (now Belleisle) on Lough Erne, controlled the shipping and fishing on the lake. Cathal Óg MacManus (1439–1498), Chief of the Name, dean of Lough Erne and vicar-general of the diocese of Clogher, was responsible for the compilation of the *Annals of Ulster*. Today the surname is most common by far in its original homelands, and especially in Co. Fermanagh. Other variants of the name in Ulster include Mayne, Moyne and, in Tyrone, Manasses.

Placenames reflecting the presence of the family are found principally in the areas of their traditional influence in the west and north: Catronmacmanus in Killasser in Co. Mayo, Annaghmacmanus in Loughgall in Armagh, Knockmacmanus in Aghavea in Fermanagh, and Lismacmanus in Rathcline in Longford.

Famous Names

TERENCE BELLEW MACMANUS (1823–1860)

A native of Fermanagh who was transported for his part in the Young Ireland rising and escaped to America from Tasmania. His funeral, in Dublin, was the occasion of one of the largest Fenian demonstrations.

ANNA MACMANUS (ETHNA CARBERY) (1866–1902)

Anna MacManus née Johnston wrote under the name Ethna Carbery. A prolific and popular poet, she founded *The Northern Patriot* and was a passionate supporter of the original Sinn Féin.

FRANCIS MACMANUS (1909–1965)

born in Kilkenny, Francis MacManus published eleven novels between 1937 and 1959, as well as numerous short stories, biographies, essays and travel books. He is best remembered for his finest book, *The Fire in the Dust* (1950).

DECLAN MACMANUS (b. 1950)

This London-born son of Irish emigrants is better known as Elvis Costello, one of the most original and influential songwriters of his generation.

MacNally

HERALDIC BLAZON
Gules an arm in armour proper garnished or and embowed couped at the shoulder holding in the hand a battle-axe of the second between six martlets argent three and three palewise, in the centre chief point an ancient Irish crown or

MacNally, MacAnally and Nally all share the same Irish origins, in the two Irish names Mac an Fhailghigh, 'son of the poor man', and Mac Con Uladh, 'son of the hound of Ulster'. As might be expected, the latter name is almost entirely confined to Ulster, in particular to that part of the modern province originally called Uladh, the south-east, including most of what are now counties Armagh and Monaghan. Today, the anglicised versions of the name remain very common in these counties, with the 'Mac-' forms in the majority. Outside Ulster, the principal origin of the name is in northwest Connacht, in counties Roscommon and Mayo, where it is said that the name was adopted by the descendants of Norman settlers. The most common form in these counties is the simple 'Nally'.

In 1890, McNally was concentrated in counties Antrim, Armagh and Monaghan (MacNally was among the twenty most common names in Monaghan in 1970), while Nally was almost exclusive to Roscommon and Mayo. Traces of the family are found in the placenames of the north and west, with Ballymacanally in Magheralin parish in Co. Down, Cahermacanally in Killursa in Co. Galway and Tanmacnally in Ematris in Co. Monaghan. Occasional variants of the name have included MacAnnuly, MacAnnulla, Knally and Manally.

DEMOGRAPHIC DATA

TRADITIONAL FAMILY AREAS
Armagh, Down, Mayo, Monaghan,
Roscommon

FAMILY RANKING
1890: 180th *1996*: 175th

NO. OF BIRTHS
1890: 121

Famous Names

REVEREND DAVID RICE MACANALLY (1810–1895)

One extremely prominent bearer of the name was the Reverend David Rice MacAnally, a sheriff and Methodist preacher who is said to have weighed more than 360 lbs.

RAY MCANALLY (1926–1989)

Ray McAnally was one of the most gifted Irish actors of his generation. He was a member of the Abbey company from 1947 to 1963 and later pursued a very successful film career, appearing in such films as *The Mission*, *Shake Hands with the Devil*, *We're No Angels* and *Billy Budd*.

DERMOT NALLY (b. 1927)

One of Ireland's most influential civil servants of the twentieth century. He acted as secretary to the government from 1980 to 1993, negotiated Irish entry into the European Monetary System, and headed the team which negotiated the 1985 Anglo–Irish Agreement.

MacNamara

HERALDIC BLAZON
Gules a lion rampant
argent, in chief two
spearheads or

MacNamara comes from the Irish Mac Conmara, 'son of the hound of the sea'. The surname arose in Co. Clare, where the family were part of the famous Dál gCais tribal grouping. They were second only to the O'Briens, to whom they were hereditary marshals. From relatively minor beginnings, they grew in power to become rulers of the territory of Clancullen, a territory including a large part of what is now east Clare, where they held sway for almost six centuries down to the final defeat of Gaelic culture in the seventeenth century. They were divided into two septs, the MacNamara Fionn ('Fair') ruling the west of the territory and the MacNamara Reagh ('Dark') ruling the east. In the course of their lordship they built dozens of castles, forts and abbeys, including two of the most famous castles in Ireland, Bunratty Castle and Knappogue Castle, both completely restored and in use as banqueting halls. They also built Quin Abbey. Today, the surname is widespread throughout Ireland, but the largest concentration remains in the area of the original homeland, in counties Clare and Limerick.

DEMOGRAPHIC DATA

TRADITIONAL FAMILY AREAS
Clare

FAMILY RANKING
1890: 94th *1996*: 115th

NO. OF BIRTHS
1890: 192

Famous Names

JAMES MACNAMARA (1768–1826)

A native of Clare who was an officer in the British navy during the Napoleonic Wars and became an admiral in 1814.

FRANCIS MACNAMARA (1885–1962)

Air Vice-Marshal of the Australian Flying Corps.

BRINSLEY MACNAMARA (1890–1963)

Novelist and playwright, and the most famous modern bearer of the surname, was in fact John Weldon. He adopted the pseudonym as protection; his most famous work, *The Valley of the Squinting Windows*, was highly critical of Irish life.

ROBERT MACNAMARA

US Secretary of Defense from 1961 to 1968 and president of the World Bank from 1968 to 1981.

MacSweeny

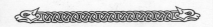

HERALDIC BLAZON
Or on a fess vert between
three boars passant sable
a lizard argent

Sweeney, along with its variants MacSweeny and MacSwiney, comes from the Irish Mac Suibhne, from *suibhne*, meaning 'pleasant. The original Suibhne from whom the surname derives was a Scottish chief based in Argyll around the year 1200. His people were of mixed Viking and Irish descent, and their fame as fighters meant that they were much in demand in Ireland as gallowglasses, or mercenaries. Suibhne's great-great-grandson Muchadh Maer Mac Suibhne settled in the Fanad district of the modern Co. Donegal in the fourteenth century, and his offspring soon split into distinct groups, the principal ones being Mac Suibhne Fanad and Mac Suibhne na dTuath. The former, senior branch, were based at Rathmullan and among their strongholds were Doe Castle and Rahan Castle. For over three centuries, up to the final defeat of the seventeenth century, they fought as gallowglasses in the struggles of Ulster, mainly on behalf of the O'Donnells. Members of both groups also made their way south to Cork in the late fifteenth century and served the MacCarthys, acquiring territory of their own in Muskerry. The Cork family prospered and multiplied, and today the surname is more numerous in the Cork/Kerry area than in its original Irish homeland of Ulster.

DEMOGRAPHIC DATA

TRADITIONAL FAMILY AREAS
Cork, Donegal

FAMILY RANKING
1890: 47th *1996*: 81st

NO. OF BIRTHS
1890: 283

Famous Names

JOHN SWINEY

A participant in both the 1798 rebellion and Robert Emmett's rising in 1803, after which he escaped to Normandy, where the family still exists.

THOMAS WILLIAM SWEENEY

A general on the Union side during the American Civil War and a member of the Fenians.

PATRICK VALENTINE MACSWINEY

Patrick Valentine MacSwiney was created a Roman hereditary marquis in 1896. He took part in the 1916 rising and later helped in the creation of the Irish diplomatic service.

TERENCE MACSWINEY (1879–1920)

One of several Cork patriots was Terence MacSwiney, the Lord Mayor of Cork who died on hunger strike in prison in 1920.

JAMES J. SWEENEY (1900–86)

Director of the New York Museum of Modern Art and a renowned art historian and critic.

Madden

HERALDIC BLAZON

Sable a falcon volant
seizing a mallard argent

Madden is the anglicised version of the Irish Ó Madaidhin, from a diminutive of *madadh*, 'hound'. The individual from whom the Maddens claim descent was Madudan, son of Gadhra Mór (d. 1008). The family were part of the Uí Maine tribal grouping based in east Co. Galway; their territory extended across the Shannon into what is now Co. Offaly. Madden strongholds are recorded at Meelick, Cloghan, in Co. Offaly, and Derryhivenny, near Portumna. Their hegemony was not seriously challenged until the English incursions of the sixteenth century when Lord Deputy Sussex captured Meelick Castle in 1557. It was destroyed in 1595, as was Cloghan Castle, in a bloody campaign which resulted in the death of many of the O'Maddens. They retained power until the final confiscations of the late seventeenth century – Derryhivenny was built as late as 1643 – but had lost all by the start of the eighteenth century. Nonetheless the family remained numerous in the area, and even today, the surname is by far most frequent in east Galway.

A branch of the family moved south to the Clare/Limerick region early on, anglicising their name as Madigan, and this separate surname is also still most strongly associated with its original homeland.

Other Maddens from Oxfordshire settled in Kildare in the sixteenth century, giving their name to Maddenstown village; debate continues whether the family were really descended from Irish emigrants.

The family name is inscribed in their local placenames: Claremadden in Kilquain and Gortymadden in Abbeygormacan, both in Co. Galway, and Carrigmadden in Youghalarra, in nearby Tipperary.

DEMOGRAPHIC DATA

TRADITIONAL FAMILY AREAS
Galway

FAMILY RANKING
1890: 211th *1996*: 202nd

NO. OF BIRTHS
1890: 107

Famous Names

RICHARD ROBERT MADDEN (1798–1886)

The most famous bearer of the name. Doctor, traveller, historian and fervent opponent of the slave trade, as well as author of the monumental and hagiographic seven-volume *The United Irishmen: their lives and times* (1842–1846).

THOMAS MORE MADDEN (1844–1902)

His son Thomas More Madden was also a well-known writer.

Maguire

HERALDIC BLAZON
Vert a white horse fully
caparisoned thereon a knight
in complete armour on his
helmet a plume of ostrich
feathers his right hand
brandishing a sword all proper

Maguire, with its variants MacGuire, McGwire, etc., comes from the Irish Mag Uidhir, meaning 'son of the brown (-haired) one'. The surname is now common throughout Ireland and especially in Cavan, Monaghan and Fermanagh; in Fermanagh it is the single most numerous name in the county. The reason is not far to seek. From the time of their first firm establishment, in Lisnaskea around the start of the thirteenth century, all the associations of the family have been with Fermanagh. By the start of the fourteenth century, the chief of the family, Donn Carrach Maguire, was ruler of the entire county, and for the next three hundred years there were no less than fifteen Maguire chieftains of the territory. By 1600, what is now Co. Fermanagh quite simply belonged to the family.

As for many other Gaelic families, however, the seventeenth century was catastrophic for the Maguires. First, a junior branch, based around the area of modern Enniskillen, were dispossessed and their lands parcelled out in the Ulster Plantation. Then, after their rebellions in the Cromwellian and Williamite periods, virtually all the rest of their Fermanagh possessions were taken. Subsequently, many Maguires took part in the migration of the native aristocracy to mainland Europe in the early eighteenth century; bearers of the name were especially prominent in the armies of France and Austria.

Unlike most of the Irish aristocracy, the Maguire descent remained intact. The current 'Maguire of Fermanagh' is Terence Maguire, officially recognised by the Chief Herald of Ireland in 1991.

DEMOGRAPHIC DATA

TRADITIONAL FAMILY AREAS
Fermanagh

FAMILY RANKING
1890: 37th   *1996*: 44th

NO. OF BIRTHS
1890: 322

Famous Names

JOHN FRANCIS MAGUIRE (1815–1872)

Among the many famous Maguires in Irish history, one of the most interesting was John Francis Maguire, founder of the *Cork Examiner*, still the most important provincial newspaper in the country. As well as a journalist, he was also a successful politician, Lord Mayor and MP for Cork for many years. He published numerous books, including *The Irish in America*, the first examination of the position of his fellow countrymen in Canada and the US.

Maher

HERALDIC BLAZON
Azure two lions rampant
combatant or supporting a
sword argent pommel and
hilt of the second, in base
two crescents of the third

Maher, and its principal variant Meagher, are the anglicised versions of the Irish Ó Meachair, from *meachar*, meaning 'hospitable'. The surname originated in Ikerrin near the modern town of Roscrea in north Tipperary, where the family retained their traditional lands right up to the modern period, resisting the encroachments of the Norman Butlers. The name remains very strongly linked to the traditional homeland, with the bulk of present-day Mahers living or originating in Co. Tipperary. Formerly pronounced as two syllables, as the Irish original would suggest, the name is now more often pronounced as a single syllable.

By 1890, Maher was one of the 100 most common names in Ireland, with the bulk of the births recorded in Tipperary and the adjoining county of Kilkenny.

DEMOGRAPHIC DATA

TRADITIONAL FAMILY AREAS
Tipperary

FAMILY RANKING
1890: 85th   *1996*: 78th

NO. OF BIRTHS
1890: 203

Famous Names

CAPTAIN JOHN MEAGHER (d. 1690)

One of the most famous casualties of the seventeenth century wars in Ireland. Having taken to a life of outlawry, he was finally captured and hanged in 1690.

THOMAS FRANCIS MEAGHER (1823–1867)

A founder of the nationalist Young Ireland movement and a man with an eventful life. Transported to Australia, he managed to escape to the USA, where he became Brigadier-General of the Irish Brigade of the Union Army during the Civil War, and was later Governor of Montana.

LORY MEAGHER (1899–1973)

One of the best hurlers of all time, he won three All-Ireland medals with his county, Kilkenny, in 1932, 1933 and 1935.

T. J. MAHER (b. 1922)

A prominent public figure for more than twenty years, T. J. Maher has been president of the Irish Farmers' Association, the Irish Co-op Society and a member of the European Parliament.

Malone

HERALDIC BLAZON
Vert a lion rampant or
between three mullets
argent

Malone is the anglicised form of the Irish Ó Maoil Eoin, meaning 'descendant of a devotee of (St) John', *maol* being the Irish for 'bald' and referring to the distinctive tonsure sported by Irish monks, and Eoin the Irish version of the Latin Ioannes. The family was an offshoot of the O'Connors of Connacht, and lived up to the ecclesiastical origin of their surname in their extended connection with the famous Abbey of Clonmacnoise, with a long line of Malone bishops and abbots. The family were also known as soldiers, with distinguished members fighting in the army of James II. After his defeat, they had to seek refuge on the continent, particularly in France and Spain.

One branch of the family, the Malones of Westmeath, retained large estates and became members of the Anglo-Irish gentry. Richard Malone (1738–1816) of this family became the first and only Lord Sunderlin.

Today the Malones are largely dispersed from their original homeland, and the highest concentrations are to be found in counties Clare and Wexford. There is some suspicion that the Clare Malones, concentrated in the east of the county, are in fact Ó Maoldúin, more often anglicised as Muldoon, since the Ó Maoldúin were well known in the area, but Muldoon is now extremely rare there.

DEMOGRAPHIC DATA

TRADITIONAL FAMILY AREAS
Galway, Roscommon

FAMILY RANKING
1890: 230th *1996*: 218th

NO. OF BIRTHS
1890:100

Famous Names

EDMUND MALONE (1741–1812)

The most famous bearer of the name was this member of the Westmeath family. He was a friend of Samuel Johnson, James Boswell, and Edmund Burke among others, and his complete edition of the works of Shakespeare remained standard for almost a century. His portrait was painted by Joshua Reynolds.

SYLVESTER MALONE (1822–1906)

A Catholic priest best remembered now for his *Church History of Ireland*, which became a standard work of reference.

WALTER MALONE (1866–1915)

Remembered as the author of a celebrated verse saga of the history of the Mississippi.

PAUL MULDOON (b. 1951)

The leading Irish poet of his generation. For many years a producer with the BBC in Belfast, he now teaches at Princeton University.

Martin

HERALDIC BLAZON

Azure a cross calvary on
three grieces argent, the
dexter arm terminating in a
sun in splendour or, the
sinister in a decrescent argent

M artin is an extremely common name throughout the English-speaking world and, in its many variant forms, throughout Europe, stemming from a diminutive of the Latin Martius, the god of war. Its popularity is largely due to the widespread fame of the fourth-century saint, Martin of Tours. In Ireland, the surname may be of English, Scottish or native Irish origin. The best-known Martins, powerful in west Galway and Galway city for centuries, were of English extraction, having arrived with the Normans. They claim descent from Oliver Martin who fought in the Crusades. The largest number of Irish origin stem from the Mac Giolla Mhairtín, 'son of the follower of (St) Martin', also anglicised as Gilmartin, who were a branch of the O'Neills. They originally held territory in the barony of Clogher in Co. Tyrone, but were displaced westwards into the adjoining counties of Sligo and Leitrim where they are most numerous today. In Scotland, the name originated from Mac Gille Mhartainn, which was first anglicised MacMartin, and then Martin. Martins were one of the three principal branches of the Clan Cameron; there was a separate family, based in Skye, who were part of the Clan Donald.

A large majority of Martins in Ireland in 1890, almost 60%, were based in Ulster, suggesting a Scottish origin for most Irish Martins.

Famous Names

RICHARD MARTIN

Richard Martin ('Nimble Dick') was the source of the family fortune of the Martins of Galway. He seized vast tracts of land in west Galway from the O'Flahertys in the great land transfers of the seventeenth century.

RICHARD MARTIN ('HUMANITY DICK') (1754–1834)

His great-grandson, also Richard Martin ('Humanity Dick'), was one of the most famous members of the family. He was a passionate supporter of animal welfare – hence the nickname, given to him by the Prince Regent – and was one of the founders of the Royal Society for the Prevention of Cruelty to Animals.

JOHN MARTIN (1812–75)

Born in Newry, Co. Down, John Martin was brother-in-law and political ally of John Mitchel, the founder of the *United Irishman*. He was transported to Tasmania for his political activities. On his return to Ireland he was elected a Home Rule MP for Meath. He was known throughout the country as Honest John Martin.

Meehan

HERALDIC BLAZON

Gules on a chevron argent
three bucks' heads erased of
the field attired or, in base a
demi-lion rampant argent

Meehan, along with its variant Meighan, comes from the Irish Ó Miadhacháin, from *miadhach*, meaning 'honourable'. Historically, the most notable family of the name were an offshoot of the MacCarthys of the kingdom of Desmond in south Munster. However, as early as the eleventh century, they migrated north to Co. Leitrim. From there they spread slowly into the adjoining counties, and are now numerous throughout east Connacht, Donegal and Fermanagh. This family preserved a sixth-century manuscript of St Molaise of Devenish from generation to generation for more than a thousand years; it is now held in the National Museum in Dublin.

There also appears to have been a separate family which adopted the surname, in the Clare/Galway region, where the name is also numerous. In Monaghan, and there alone, it has been anglicised as Meegan. In Sligo the name Ó Maotháin has sometimes been anglicised as Meehan, while in east Ulster MacMeekin, from the Irish Mac Miadhacháin, has also sometimes become Meehan.

The presence of the family is recorded in the names of the places associated with them: Lismeehan in Tulla parish and Rathmeehan in Killone in Co. Clare, Killymeehan in Larah in Co. Cavan, Cloonameehan in Killoghill, Co. Sligo.

Famous Names

JAMES MEEHAN

A co-explorer with Hamilton Hume on his pioneering explorations of the Australian interior in the early nineteenth century.

COUNT JAMES ANTHONY MEHEGAN (1719–1792)

A member of the family – the surname is a closer phonetic rendering of the original Irish – and a famous soldier in the Irish Brigade in the French army.

ITA MEEHAN (b. 1922)

One of very few women to have reached the upper levels of the Irish civil service. She was highly influential in the development of the telecommunications sector, which was crucial to the rapid development of the country in the 1990s.

PAULA MEEHAN (b. 1955)

Paula Meehan is among the most powerful and most popular of the younger generation of Irish poets. Her best-known collection is *The Man Marked by Winter* (1991).

Molloy

HERALDIC BLAZON

Argent a lion rampant
sable between three
trefoils slipt gules

Molloy, with Mulloy and O'Molloy, is the anglicised version of a number of distinct Irish names. The Ó Maolmhuaidh, from *maolmhuadh*, meaning 'proud chieftain', in earlier times anglicised as O'Mulmoy, were part of the southern Uí Néill, the southern branch of the large tribal grouping claiming descent from Niall of the Nine Hostages, the fifth-century king who supposedly kidnapped St Patrick to Ireland. They held power over the ancient kingdom of Fercal, covering much of modern Co. Offaly, where the surname is still very common. The family were prominent in the early English administration of Ireland. One of their number, then bishop of Ferns, helped to officiate at the coronation of Richard I (although he later excommunicated the Earl of Pembroke) and the chief of the family became hereditary standard bearer for the English in Ireland.

A second family were the Ó Maoil Aodha, 'descendant of the devotee of (St) Aodh', from *maol*, literally 'bald', a reference to the distinctive tonsure sported by early Irish monks. As well as Molloy, this surname has also been anglicised as Mullee. The name arose in east Connacht, in the Roscommon/east Galway region, and remains numerous there today.

In Ulster Ó Maolmhaodhóg, 'descendant of the devotee of (St) Maodhóg', more usually rendered into English as Mulvogue, or Logue, has been confused with Molloy, particularly around the Glenties area. Molloy is now common there.

In 1890 the name was concentrated in counties Donegal, Dublin, Galway and Mayo.

Famous Names

JAMES LYNAM MOLLOY (1837–1909)

was a composer of popular ballads, many of which are still sung. *Love's Old Sweet Song* is the best known example of his work.

M. J. MOLLOY (1917–1994)

A small farmer near Milltown, Co. Galway, who was also a successful playwright. Many of his plays, including his best-known, *The Wood of the Whispering*, were produced by the Abbey Theatre in the 1930s and '40s. They enjoyed a revival in the 1980s, in the Druid Theatre.

BOBBY MOLLOY (b. 1936)

A politician and member of Dáil Éireann, the Irish parliament, for over thirty years. He has been a minister in four governments and was one of the founders of the Progressive Democrats in 1986.

Moloney

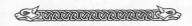

HERALDIC BLAZON
Azure, on the dexter side
a quiver of three arrows, on
the sinister a bow erect all or

Moloney, along with its variants Mullowney and Maloney, is the English version of Ó Maol Dhomnaigh, meaning 'descendant of the servant of the church'. *Maol* means 'bald', and refers to the distinctive tonsure common in the early Irish Church, while *domhnach* means 'Sunday', and was used by extension to refer to the place of worship on that day. The surname arose in Co. Clare, near the modern town of Tulla, and remains extremely common there, as well as in the adjoining counties of Limerick and Tipperary.

Mullowney has also sometimes been used as the anglicisation of the Ulster surname Mac Giolla Dhomnaigh, meaning 'son of the servant of the church', usually anglicised as Downey or MacEldowney, which is found principally in counties Antrim and Derry. Both of these name were sometimes used for the illegitimate offspring of clergymen.

In addition Ó Maolfhachtna, a north Tipperary name, is now generally found as Moloney, perhaps reflecting the proximity of the Clare family. Other, rare, anglicisations of this name include Loughney and MacLoughney.

Ó Maolanfaidh, a Cork name usually rendered Molumby, is also on occasion found as Moloney.

The Moloney family are represented in the placenames of their home territory, with Ballymoloney in Killokennedy parish in Clare and Feenagh (Moloney) in Feenagh parish in the same county.

Famous Names

MARTIN MOLONY (1847–1929)

An emigrant who made his fortune in the USA and devoted much of his wealth to good causes.

HELENA MOLONY (1884–1967)

Helena Molony was a feminist, a revolutionary and a trade unionist. After the political struggles of the early years of the century she fought on the Anti-treaty side in the Civil War. In 1936 she was elected president of the Trades Union Congress.

Monaghan

HERALDIC BLAZON
Azure a chevron between
three mullets or

Monaghan (or Monahan) is the English version of the Irish Ó Manacháin, from a diminutive of *manach*, meaning 'monk', and some of the family adopted the semi-translation Monks or Monk. Most of the surname in Ireland descend from one Manacháin, a chieftain who lived in Connacht in the ninth century, and it is with that province, specifically with east Roscommon close to the River Shannon, that the family are most closely linked. Up to the end of the thirteenth century they were rulers of this area, known as 'The Three Tuathas'. The name has spread from the original homeland, and is now common also is Mayo and Galway.

In Co. Fermanagh, where the name is also numerous, the family are thought to be part of the original inhabitants of the area, the Fir Manach, from whom the county gets its name. Their base was in the district of Lurg. From here the name has now also spread into the adjoining counties of Monaghan and Derry.

In 1890, the name was concentrated in Galway, Mayo and Fermanagh.

TRADITIONAL FAMILY AREAS
Fermanagh, Roscommon

FAMILY RANKING
1890: 150th   *1996*: 151st

BIRTHS
1890: 140

Famous Names

JAMES HENRY MONAGHAN (1804–1878)

The Galway-born became Lord Chief Justice of Ireland who was
responsible for the prosecutions of the Young Irelanders and
the Fenians.

PHILIP MONAHAN (1894–1983)

A participant in the War of Independence, he afterwards became an
influential civil servant. He was appointed City Manager of Cork
for life at the age of 35.

RINTY MONAGHAN (1920–1984)

The Belfast boxer who became world flyweight champion in 1947 and
retired undefeated in 1949, suffering from tuberculosis.

Mooney

HERALDIC BLAZON

Argent a holly tree eradicated vert thereon a lizard passant or, a border compony counter compony of the first and second

Mooney comes from the Irish Ó Maonaigh, which may derive from the Old Irish *moenach*, meaning 'dumb', or from *maonach*, meaning 'wealthy'. It arose as a surname independently in each of the four provinces.

In Ulster it was the name of a family based in the parish of Ardara, in Co. Donegal, who were hereditary holders of the church lands of Shanaghan. The eponymous ancestor was Monach, son of Ailloll Mór. Other variant anglicisations in this area include Moany and Money.

The Connacht family were located in the parish of Easky in the barony of Tireragh in Co. Sligo, where Meeny is often the English version used. In Munster, reflecting the different pronunciation, the English is often Mainey. But the most notable family arose in Leinster, in the modern Co. Offaly, where they were concentrated around the parish of Lemanaghan. They were hereditary guardians of the shrine of St Monaghan. Their descendants are by far the most numerous today, although the name has now spread throughout Ireland.

The Sligo family gave their name to the townland of Ballymeeny in Easky parish. The Offaly family are very well represented, with Ballymooneys in Offaly, Laois and Wicklow, as well as Mooneysland, also in Offaly, and two Mooneystowns and a Knockmooney in Meath.

In Munster, where the name is more uncommon, Ó Maonaigh was generally anglicised as Mainey, reflecting its southern pronunciation.

DEMOGRAPHIC DATA

TRADITIONAL FAMILY AREAS
Donegal, Offaly, Sligo

FAMILY RANKING
1890: 158th *1996*: 111th

NO. OF BIRTHS
1890: 136

Famous Names

WILLIAM MOONEY

The subsequently infamous Tammany Hall was founded in New York City in 1789 by William Mooney, a former soldier and a prominent anti-Federalist.

DONAGH MOONEY

An Irish Franciscan who was guardian of the young O'Neill, Earl of Tyrone and O'Donnell, Earl of Tirconnell at Louvain in 1626.

RIA MOONEY (1904–1973)

An actress who joined the Abbey Theatre in 1924 and played the lead in the first production of *The Plough and the Stars*. She went on to produce and direct in New York and, back in Dublin from the 1940s, in the Gate, the Abbey and the Gaiety.

Moran

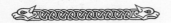

HERALDIC BLAZON
Sable three stars rayed or

Moran is the anglicisation of a number of distinct Irish names. Ó Moráin, from a diminutive of *mór*, meaning 'big', (which makes the name, roughly translated, Little Big Man) arose in Co. Mayo, near the modern town of Ballina, where the eponymous ancestor Moráin held power. Another family with the same name, part of the Muintir Eolais, were based in Co. Leitrim.

Ó Mughráin – the origins of the name remain unclear – was also the name of two distinct Connacht families. One was a minor branch of the Uí Maine tribal grouping, based around Criffon in Co. Galway. The other were related to the O'Connors of Connacht and based near the modern village of Elphin in north Roscommon.

Ó Murcháin, from *murchadha*, 'sea-warrior', is now generally anglicised Moran, though it has been rendered as Morahan and Morrin. The family were originally of east Offaly, near the Co. Kildare border.

Last but not least come the Mac Moruinn of Fermanagh, whose name is anglicised Moran, MacMoran and MacMorrinn.

Unsurprisingly, the vast majority of Morans are of Connacht origin, with particular concentrations in Leitrim, Mayo and Roscommon. As might be expected, the presence of these families is well recorded in the placenames of their territories, with an Ardmoran and Lismoran in Mayo, Caldrymoran in Roscommon, two Ballymorans in Offaly, Killormoran in Galway and Rathmoran in Fermanagh.

DEMOGRAPHIC DATA

TRADITIONAL FAMILY AREAS
Fermanagh, Galway, Mayo, Offaly,
Roscommon

FAMILY RANKING
1890: 53rd   *1996*: 71st

NO. OF BIRTHS
1890: 265

Famous Names

MICHAEL MORAN (1794–1856)

One of the most famous bearers of the name was actually better known
by his nickname of Zozimus. He was blinded in infancy and made his
living on the streets of Dublin with his recitations and ballads. A
monument to him stands in Glasnevin cemetery.

FRANCES MORAN (1893–1977)

The first Irishwoman ever to become a Senior Counsel. She was also the
first woman Professor at Trinity College Dublin, and the first woman on
the board of the college.

KEVIN MORAN (b. 1954)

The only sportsperson ever to win both All-Ireland Gaelic football medals
(with Dublin in 1976 and 1977) and English FA Cup medals (with
Manchester United in 1983 and 1985).

Moriarty

HERALDIC BLAZON
Argent an eagle
displayed sable

Moriarty is the English version of the Irish Ó Muircheartaigh, made up of *muir*, 'sea', and *ceardach*, 'skilled'; 'one skilled in the ways of the sea'. The name is undoubtedly linked to their original homeland, on both sides of Castlemaine harbour in south Co. Kerry. The continuity of their association with the area is remarkable, even by Irish standards. They have lived in the area since the surname came into being in the eleventh century, and 90% of present births of the surname are still in Co. Kerry. This continuity is all the more tenacious for the fact that they had lost virtually all of their power in the area by the fourteenth century. Ó Muircheartaigh was also a surname found in Meath and the midlands, but in these areas it has been anglicised as Murtagh. Murtagh is also the anglicisation commonly found in Ulster for Ó Muircheartaigh, though it has also been given as Murdoch, by association with the common Scottish name.

The presence of the original Ó Muircheartaigh in the north is reflected in placenames, with Killymoriarty in Co. Armagh and Kilmoriarty in Co. Cavan.

Famous Names

PATRICK MORIARTY (1804–1875)

The famous American preacher and temperance reformer was born in Dublin of a Kerry family.

DAVID MORIARTY (1814–1877)

A Catholic bishop of Kerry notorious for his vehement denunciations of all opposition to the British government, saying of the Fenian leaders 'eternity is not long enough nor Hell hot enough for such miscreants.'

MICHEÁL Ó MUIRCHEARTAIGH

One of the best-known sports broadcasters in Ireland. His distinctive Kerry tones are an essential feature of All-Ireland finals.

PROFESSOR MORIARTY

Professor Moriarty was the evil creation of Sir Arthur Conan Doyle, and was Sherlock Holmes' fiendishly clever arch-opponent.

Morris

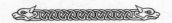

HERALDIC BLAZON

Or a fess dancetée, in base a lion rampant sable

Morris is a common surname throughout the British Isles, and in virtually all cases is derived, directly or indirectly, from the personal name Maurice, which comes from the Latin *maurus*, meaning 'moorish'. A large number of those bearing the name in Ireland, where the name is most frequent in Leinster, with significant numbers also in Ulster and Connacht, will be of English, Scottish or Welsh origin.

There was also an Irish family, the Ó Muirgheasa (from *muir*, 'sea' and *geasa*, 'taboo') part of the Uí Fiachraigh tribal grouping in Co. Sligo, whose surname was originally anglicised Morrissey, and later shortened to Morris. Ó Muirgheasa was also the surname of a family in Co. Fermanagh who anglicised their name to Morris. The most prominent family of the name, one of the famous 'Tribes of Galway', were of Norman extraction and originally known as de Marreis or de Marisco. The arms are for this family.

In addition, the Norman Fitzmaurice (in Irish Mac Muiris) has often been abbreviated to Morris. The Fitzmaurices were a branch of the Geraldines, very well known and still very numerous in their homeland near Lixnaw in Kerry. They were prominent in the resistance to the incursions of the English in the sixteenth century.

DEMOGRAPHIC DATA

TRADITIONAL FAMILY AREAS
Fermanagh, Kerry, Sligo

FAMILY RANKING
1890: 196th   *1996*: 182nd

NO. OF BIRTHS
1890: 115

Famous Names

JAMES FITZMAURICE (1898–1965)

James Fitzmaurice became Commandant of the Irish Air Corps in 1927, and in 1928, together with his German co-pilot Captain Koehl, made the first east-to-west transatlantic flight.

MICHAEL MORRIS, LORD KILLANIN (b. 1914)

Lord Killanin has had a long and distinguished career as a journalist and businessman but is best known for his work with the International Olympic Committee, of which he was president from 1970 to 1980.

GABRIEL FITZMAURICE (b. 1952)

A teacher in his native Kerry, a distinguished poet in both Irish and English and a recorded singer and performer, as well as one of the main driving forces behind the annual Listowel Writers' Week.

Mullan

HERALDIC BLAZON

Argent a dexter hand couped at the wrist in fess gules holding a dagger in pale proper between three crescents gules

Mullan, together with its variants Mullin, Mullen, Mullane and Mullins, can have a variety of distinct origins. First, it may be the anglicisation of the Irish name Ó Maoláin, from a diminutive of *maol*, 'bald' or 'tonsured', which arose separately in a number of areas. The Co. Galway family of the name claim descent from Maolán, himself descended from a king of Connacht. A different family of the same name were based in the Keenaght district of Co. Derry, having originally lived in the Laggan district of Donegal, and were followers of the O'Cahans. In Co. Monaghan a family of the name arose around the modern town of Clones; their name has also been anglicised as Mollins. In nearby Tyrone, the Ó Mealláin, more accurately anglicised as O'Mellan or Mellon, have become Mullans in many instances, no doubt because of the numerical superiority and resultant familiarity of the latter. Yet another family hails from south Co. Cork, where the name is frequently given as Mullins. As well as all of these, many MacMillans, Scottish settlers in Ulster in the seventeenth century, adopted MacMullan, often shortened to Mullan. There is also an English name Mullins, from the Middle English *miln*, 'mill', and a good number of Irish bearers of the name are undoubtedly of this origin.

DEMOGRAPHIC DATA

TRADITIONAL FAMILY AREAS
Cork, Derry, Donegal, Galway,
Monaghan, Tyrone

FAMILY RANKING
1890: 71st *1996*: 88th

NO. OF BIRTHS
1890: 218

Famous Names

ALAN MULLAN (d. 1690)

The well-known anatomist who discovered the circulatory system of the
eye when he dissected an elephant in 1681.

SHANE CROSAGH O'MULLAN

Shane Crosagh O'Mullan, of the Derry family, lost his property in 1729
and subsequently became a notorious outlaw, or rapparee. He was
eventually captured and hanged, along with his two sons, at Derry.

KARL MULLEN (b. 1926)

A member of the Munster family who was one of Ireland's best rugby
players. He captained the Irish team to its only Grand Slam in 1948.

Murphy

HERALDIC BLAZON

Quarterly argent and gules,
on a fess sable between four
lions rampant counter-
changed three garbs or

Murphy is the anglicised version of two Irish surnames, Ó Murchadha (in modern Irish Ó Murchú) and Mac Murchadha, both derived from the popular early Irish personal name Murchadh, 'sea-warrior'. Mac Murchadha (son of Murchadh) is exclusive to Ulster, where the family were part of the Cenél Eoghain, the tribal grouping claiming descent from Eoghan, himself a son of the fifth century founder of the Uí Néill dynasty, Niall of the Nine Hostages. These Ulster Murphys (or MacMuphys) were originally based in present-day Co. Tyrone, in the area known as Muintir Birn, but were driven out by the O'Neills and settled in south Armagh, where they were subjects of the O'Neills of the Fews. In Ulster today, Murphy remains most numerous in Co. Armagh, though it is also to be found in great numbers in Fermanagh and Monaghan.

Elsewhere in Ireland, Ó Murchadha (descendant of Murchadh) is the original Irish. This arose separately in at least three distinct areas – Cork, Roscommon and Wexford. The most prominent of these were the Wexford Uí Murchadha. These took their surname from Murchadh or Murrough, grandfather of Dermot MacMurrough, King of Leinster, and thus share their origin not only with the MacMurroughs but also with the Kinsellas, the Kavanaghs and the MacDavy Mores. Their territory lay in the barony of Ballaghkeen in Wexford, and was formerly known as Hy Felimy, from Felim, one of the sons of Eanna Cinnseallaigh, the semi-legendary fourth-century ruler of Leinster. Their chief seats in this area were at Morriscastle (Murchu's Castle), Toberlamina, Oulart and Oularteigh

Famous Names

CHARLES FRANCIS MURPHY (1858–1924)

The best known leader of the Democratic Party in New York when the party's power was at its peak. The period is best known now by the name of the party headquarters, Tamanny Hall.

MARIE LOUISE O MURPHY (1737–1814)

The daughter of an Irish soldier who settled at Rouen. The famous painting of her by Boucher so intrigued Louis XV that Marie Louise became his mistress.

SEAMUS MURPHY (1907–75)

A well-known sculptor, he became professor of Sculpture at the Royal Hibernian Academy. His autobiography, *Stone Mad*, is a classic.

Nolan

HERALDIC BLAZON

Argent on a cross gules a
lion passant between four
martlets of the first, in
each quarter a sword erect
of the second

Nolan (or Nowlan) is now among the most common surnames in Ireland. It the anglicised form of Ó Nualláin, from a diminutive of *nuall*, meaning 'famous' or 'noble'. The family are strongly linked with the area of the modern Co. Carlow, where, in pre-Norman times, they held power in the barony of Forth, whence their ancient title of 'Princes of Foharta'. Their power was greatly diminished after the arrival of the Normans, but the surname is still strongly linked with the area. The prevalence of the surname in the modern counties of Mayo and Galway is explained by the migration of a branch of the family to that area in the sixteenth century; in 1585 Thomas Nolan of Ballinrobe in Mayo was given large grants of land as payment for acting as Clerk of the county. He also obtained lucrative licenses to sell wine and spirits throughout the West. He and his relatives prospered and their descendants are many. There was also a separate family, in Irish Ó hUallacháin, based in west Cork, whose name was also anglicised as Nolan.

DEMOGRAPHIC DATA

TRADITIONAL FAMILY AREAS
Carlow, Cork

FAMILY RANKING
1890: 38th   *1996*: 34th

NO. OF BIRTHS
1890: 321

Famous Names

BRIAN O'NOLAN (1911–1966)

The most famous modern bearer of this surname in Ireland was better known under his two pen-names of Flann O'Brien and Myles na Gopaleen, whose genius for comic invention has only been fully appreciated since his death. His best-known work is *At Swim-Two-Birds*.

SIR SIDNEY NOLAN (1917–1992)

One of the best artists of his generation, and the first Australian painter to become internationally famous. In acknowledgment of his Irish roots, he donated a large collection of his paintings to Ireland in 1986.

CHRISTOPHER NOLAN (b. 1965)

Christopher Nolan was born quadriplegic and language-impaired but has had a remarkable literary career. His autobiography *Under the Eye of the Clock* won the Whitbread Prize in 1988.

O'Brien

HERALDIC BLAZON
Gules three lions passant
guardant in pale per pale
or and argent

Ó Brien is in Irish O'Briain, from the personal name Brian. Its meaning is problematic, possibly deriving from *bran*, 'raven', or, more likely, from Brion, taken from the Celtic ancestor of Welsh in which *bre-* means 'hill' or 'high place'. By association, the name would then mean 'lofty' or 'eminent'.

Whatever the word's initial meaning, the historic origin of the surname containing it is clear: it denotes a descendant of Brian Ború, (Brian of the Tributes), High King in 1002 and victor at the Battle of Clontarf in 1014. He was a member of the relatively obscure Ui Toirdealbhaigh, part of the Dál gCais tribal grouping based in the Clare/Limerick area. Having secured control of the Dál gCais in 976, he defeated and killed the Eoghanacht king of Munster two years later, and proceeded to wage war against the kingdoms of Connacht, Meath, Leinster and Breifne. Eventually he won submission and tributes from all but the northern Uí Néill, the Leinstermen and the Vikings. His victory at Clontarf united Ireland, nominally at least, under a single leader, though he himself was slain. It is not surprising that his harp became the model for Ireland's national emblem.

The first individual clearly to use O'Brien as a hereditary surname was Donogh Cairbre O'Brien, son of the king of Munster, Donal Mor. His descendants spilt into a number of branches, including the O'Briens of Aherlow, the O'Briens of Waterford, the O'Briens of Arra in north Tipperary, and the O'Briens of Limerick, where the surname is perpetuated in the name of the barony of Pubblebrien.

TRADITIONAL FAMILY AREAS
Clare, Limerick

FAMILY RANKING
1890: 10th   *1996*: 8th

NO. OF BIRTHS
1890: 502

Famous Names

WILLIAM SMITH O'BRIEN (1803–1864)

William Smith O'Brien was one of the founders of the Young Ireland movement, and took a prominent part in the rising on 1848.

DERMOD O'BRIEN (1865–1945)

The grandson of William Smith O'Brien, he was a leading portrait painter in Dublin for almost forty years.

KATE O'BRIEN (1897–1954)

Novelist and dramatist who suffered, like most Irish novelists of worth, at the hands of the censors in the early years of the Irish Free State.

O'Callaghan

HERALDIC BLAZON

Argent in base a mount
vert on the dexter side a
hurst of oak trees issuant
therefrom a wolf passant
towards the sinister all proper

Along with its variants (O')Callagan, Callahan, etc., O'Callaghan comes from the Irish Ó Ceallacháin, from the personal name Ceallachán, a diminutive of *ceallach*. This was traditionally taken to mean 'frequenter of churches', but is now thought to be a much older word meaning 'bright-headed'. The personal name was favoured by the Eoghanacht, the tribal grouping who controlled the kingship of Munster before the rise of Brian Ború of the Dál gCais, and it is from one of the Eoghanacht kings, Ceallachán (d. 954) that the family trace their descent. Murchadh Ua Ceallacháin, a grandson of this king who lived in the early eleventh century, was the first to transmit the surname hereditarily.

By the end of the thirteenth century, the O'Callaghans had taken decisive possession of that part of Co. Cork which came to be known as Pobal Ui Ceallacháin, O'Callaghan's Country. This was a very large area on both sides of the River Blackwater west of the modern town of Mallow. Here their principal bases were the castles at Clonmeen and Dromaneen, and from them they retained virtually uninterrupted control for over four centuries

In the seventeenth century, the ruling chief, Donncha O'Callaghan had some 20,000 acres of land confiscated and, with his extended family, was transplanted to east Clare where he obtained land in the barony of Tulla. Despite this transplantation, most O'Callaghans remained in their ancestral homeland, largely as tenants of newly installed English owners, a few having regained possession of small parts of their old lands.

Famous Names

CORNELIUS O'CALLAGHAN

Like so many others from the old Gaelic aristocracy, members of this Clare family emigrated to continental Europe. Cornelius O'Callaghan entered the army of Spain in 1717.

DON JUAN O'CALLAGHAN

In 1944 his descendant, Don Juan O'Callaghan of Tortosa was recognised by the Genealogical Office as the senior descendant in the male line of the last inaugurated chief, the Donncha, who was transplanted to Clare.

O'Connell

HERALDIC BLAZON

Per fess argent and vert a stag trippant proper between three trefoils slipped counterchanged

Along with Connell, O'Connell generally comes from the Irish Ó Conaill, 'descendant of Conall', a very popular personal name probably derived from *con*, 'hound', and *gal*, 'valour'. Because of the widespread popularity of the personal name at its root, O'Connell arose separately as a surname in Connacht, Ulster and Munster. The native O'Connells of Ulster and Connacht have dwindled in numbers and prominence over the years, however. By far the most famous and numerous family were the O'Connells of Munster, where the family are recorded as chiefs in the barony of Magunihy in east Kerry. Driven from this area by the O'Donoghues in the eleventh century, they moved south and the centre of their power shifted to Ballycarbery, also in Co. Kerry. Their castle was destroyed in the Cromwellian wars of the mid seventeenth century. Today a large majority of the O'Connells in Ireland are still to be found in Co. Kerry, as well as in adjoining Co. Cork.

Possibly because of the fame of Daniel O'Connell, the resumption of the 'O' prefix among the family has been widespread; whereas almost 60% of the births of the name in 1890 are Connell, by 1996 only 12% of households are recorded thus.

In Ulster, especially in counties Antrim, Tyrone and Down, many Connells and MacConnells are of Scottish stock, their names derived from a phonetic transliteration of Mac Dhomhnail, since the 'Dh-' is not pronounced. This family were a branch of the great Clan Donald.

DEMOGRAPHIC DATA

TRADITIONAL FAMILY AREAS
Cork, Kerry

FAMILY RANKING
1890: 166th *1996*: 37th

NO. OF BIRTHS
1890: 130

Famous Names

DANIEL O'CONNELL (1775–1845)

The Munster family produced the most famous bearer of the name, Daniel O'Connell was known as 'The Liberator' because he won Catholics the right to sit as MPs; for almost thirty years he was the undisputed leader of Catholic Ireland.

MUIRCHERATACH O'CONNELL (1738–1830)

Muircheratach O'Connell fought with the Austrians in the Seven Year War, having changed his first name to the more acceptable 'Moritz', and became Imperial Chamberlain for more than sixty years, serving three Austrian emperors.

SIR MAURICE O'CONNELL (1766–1848)

A kinsman, Sir Maurice O'Connell served in both the French and the British armies and married a daughter of Captain Bligh of the mutinous *Bounty*. Many of his descendants still live in Australia.

MICK O'CONNELL (b. 1937)

From Valentia, Co. Kerry, Mick O'Connell is regarded as one of the finest Gaelic footballers of his generation. He won four All-Ireland medals and six National Football league medals.

O'Connor

HERALDIC BLAZON
Argent an oak tree vert

With its variants Connor, Conner, Connors, etc., O'Connor comes from the Irish Conchobhair, from the personal name Conchobhar, perhaps meaning 'lover of hounds' or 'wolf-lover'. This was a favourite early-Irish name, and gave rise to the surname in at least five distinct areas: in Connacht (O'Conor Don), in Offaly (O'Conor Faly), in north Clare (O'Conor of Corcomroe), in Keenaght in Co. Derry, and in Kerry (O'Connor Kerry).

The Offaly family take their name from Conchobhar (d. 979), who claimed descent from Cathaoir Mor, a second-century king of Ireland. They remained powerful in their original homeland until the sixteenth century, when they were dispossessed of their lands.

The O'Connor Kerry were chiefs of a large territory in north Kerry, displaced further northwards by the Norman invasion to the Limerick borders, where they retained much of their power to the seventeenth century. Today, the descendants of these O'Connors are by far the most numerous, with the majority of the many O'Connors in Ireland concentrated in the Kerry/Limerick/Cork area.

However, the most famous of the O'Connor families is that from Connacht. The ancestor from whom they take their surname was Conchobhar, King of Connacht (d. 971), and direct ancestor of the last two High Kings of Ireland, Turlough O'Connor and Roderick O'Connor, who ruled through the twelfth century. The O'Connors of Connacht retained much of their power in the seventeenth century and beyond, and the line of descent from the last Chief of the Name is also intact.

DEMOGRAPHIC DATA

TRADITIONAL FAMILY AREAS
Clare, Derry, Kerry, Offaly, Sligo,
Roscommon

FAMILY RANKING
1890: 52nd *1996*: 7th

NO. OF BIRTHS
1890: 266

Famous Names

CHARLES O'CONOR (1710–1791)

Charles O'Conor of Belanagare, of the Roscommon family, was one of
the most famous antiquarians of the eighteenth century.

RODERIC O'CONNOR (1860–1940)

Also originally from Roscommon, he was a painter who exhibited with
Van Gogh, Toulouse-Lautrec and Seurat in Paris in the 1880s, and
became a close friend of Gauguin. He followed his own path, belonging
to no school, and since his death his reputation has continued to grow.

JAMES CHARLES O'CONNOR (1853–1928)

A Corkman who settled in Germany where he became prominent in the
promotion of Esperanto. Among the many works he published was a
translation into Esperanto of the Gospel of St John.

O'Donnell

HERALDIC BLAZON

Or issuing from the sinister side of the shield an arm fessways vested azure cuffed argent holing in the and proper a passion cross gules

The surname O'Donnell comes from the Irish Ó Domhnaill, 'descendant of Domhnall', a personal name meaning 'world-mighty'. Given the nam's popularity, it is not surprising that the surname based on it arose simultaneously in a number of areas, among them west Clare and east Galway, where they were part of the Uí Máine, the sept grouping under the control of the O'Kellys. But the most famous O'Donnells are undoubtedly those based in Donegal.

Like many northern families, the O'Donnells of Tír Conaill were part of the great Uí Néill tribal grouping, claiming common descent from Niall Noigiallach, Niall of the Nine Hostages, and are the best known of the Cenél Conaill, those descended from Niall's son Conall; it is from Conall that Tír Conaill (Conall's country) derives. The O'Donnells were not prominent initially, inhabiting a small territory around Kilmacrenan. But from the late Middle Ages their power and influence grew until, by the fourteenth century, they were undisputed lords of Tír Conaill, roughly identical to modern Donegal.

Their dynasty continued for more than three centuries, culminating with their involvement in the Nine Years War, in which Red Hugh O'Donnell (1571–1602) and his brother Rory, 1st Earl of Tyrconnell (1575–1608) played a famous part, almost inflicting a decisive reverse on the progress of English rule. Their defeat marked the beginning of the end for the old Gaelic order in Ireland.

Famous Names

JAMES LOUIS O'DONNELL (1738–1811)

Prior of the Franciscans in Waterford from where he was sent to minister to the spiritual needs of the many Waterford emigrants in Newfoundland. He became known as 'the Apostle of Newfoundland'.

PEADAR O'DONNELL (1893–1986)

Writer and socialist who was Ireland's best-known and most influential dissident from the 1930s to the 1960s.

MARY O'DONNELL (b. 1954)

Regarded as one of the best contemporary Irish writers, she has published poetry, fiction and criticism.

O'Donoghue

The name (O')Donoghue, with its variants Donohue, Donahoe, Donohoe, etc., comes from the Irish Ó Donnchadha, from the popular personal name Donncha, from *donn*, meaning 'brown'. The surname would thus mean literally 'descendant of the brown-haired (or brown-complexioned) man'. The personal name's popularity meant that the surname arose independently in a number of places, including Galway/Roscommon, Cork, Tipperary and Cavan. It is especially numerous in Tipperary and in south-west Co. Cork. Generally, the anglicised versions vary only slightly, with Donohoe commoner in Galway and Cavan; one exception is in Co. Kilkenny, where the anglicisation was Dunphy.

Historically, the most important family were the O'Donoghue of Desmond, or south Munster. These were part of the Eoghanacht peoples, dominant across the south of the country until the rise of the Dál gCais under Brian Ború, and shared their ancestry with the O'Mahonys. Like the O'Mahonys, the Desmond O'Donoghues saw their power diminished by the steady rise of the MacCarthys. By the fourteenth century, they had been displaced from their original west Cork homeland, and settled in south-west Kerry where they split into two groups, the O'Donoghue Mór, based around Lough Leine near Killarney, and O'Donoghue of the Glen, based in Glenflesk.

O'Donoghue Mór, like most of the Gaelic aristocracy, were later disposessed. Their property, centred around Ross Castle, was confiscated under Elizabeth I and later granted to Sir Valentine Browne, whose family were later earls of Kenmare and viscounts Castlerosse.

DEMOGRAPHIC DATA

TRADITIONAL FAMILY AREAS
Cavan, Galway, Kerry, Roscommon,
Tipperary

FAMILY RANKING
1890: 90th   *1996*: 48th

NO. OF BIRTHS
1890: 201

Famous Names

JUAN O'DONOJU (1751–1821)

The last Spanish ruler of Mexico was descendant of an O'Donoghue emigrant to Spain.

DANIEL O'DONOGHUE OF THE GLENS (1833–89)

MP for Tipperary and a prominent nationalist.

JOHN O'DONOGHUE (1900–1964)

A novelist who wrote movingly and simply about his experience of rural Ireland.

AMERICAN O'DONOGHUES

In the US, a number of bearers of the name became well known: Peter Donahue was one of the founders of San Francisco, making his fortune from the early development of the city; Patrick Donohoe was the founder and editor of the famous *Boston Pilot* newspaper; and the Donoghues of Newburgh, New York produced three of the fastest ice-skaters in the world.

O'Driscoll

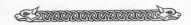

HERALDIC BLAZON
Argent an ancient galley
sails furled sable

The surname comes from the Irish Ó hEidirsceoil, grandson of Eidirsceol (from *eidirsceol*, 'go-between' or 'bearer of news'). The Eidirsceol from whom descent is claimed is said to have lived in the tenth century. Personal names of the family in its early years were Finn and Con or Mac Con, later anglicised as Florence and Cornelius.

The name is one of the very few to be clearly identified with the Érainn, or Fir Bolg, Celts who were settled in Ireland well before the arrival of the Gaels. Although the evidence is sparse, before the eighth century AD what is now Co. Cork appears to have been populated mainly by tribes of Érainn descent, including the Corca Laoighde tribal grouping of whom the Uí hEidirsceoil were the chief family. All the Érainn tribes were assimilated or displaced by the encroachment southwards of the Gaelic Eoghanacht of Cashel from the eighth century onward. The Corca Laoighde moved towards the south-west, into an area roughly defined by the modern towns of Roscarbery, Skibbereen, Schull and Baltimore. Baltimore was the seat of O'Driscolls, and gets its name (Baile an Tighe Mór) from their castle or great house.

The O'Driscolls became expert seafarers with a reputation for ferocity, but by the fifteenth century they were struggling to retain their lands and power against the English. By 1610, Baltimore was an English port, and there is evidence that the family had a hand in the notorious pillage of the town by Algerian pirates in 1631.

The O'Driscolls were ultimately dispossessed, though the family and the name remain inextricably linked to their old homeland.

DEMOGRAPHIC DATA

TRADITIONAL FAMILY AREAS
Cork

FAMILY RANKING
1890: 179th *1996*: 149th

NO. OF BIRTHS
1890: 121

Famous Names

DR KIERAN O'DRISCOLL (b. 1920)

Master of the National Maternity Hospital in Dublin from 1963 to 1969. He devised and introduced a system, *The Active Management of Labour*, now widely followed throughout the world.

DENNIS O'DRISCOLL (b. 1954)

One of Ireland's best-known contemporary poets. Apart from his four volumes of wryly personal poems, he has published much criticism and is a former editor of *Poetry Ireland Review*.

T. J. O'DRISCOLL (b. 1908)

One of the most influential Irish civil servants in the second half of the twentieth century. He played many roles, including Irish Minister to the Netherlands (1955–1956), Director-General of Bord Fáilte, the Irish Tourist Board (1956–1971) and vice-president of the Institute of Public Administration.

O'Hara

HERALDIC BLAZON
Vert on a pale radiant or
a lion rampant sable

The surname O'Hara is a phonetic anglicisation of Ó hEaghra. The family claim descent from Eaghra, lord of Luighne (the modern Leyney) in Co. Sligo, who died in 976 and who was himself, in the traditional genealogies, of the family of Olloil Ollum, king of Munster. The O'Haras remain strongly associated with Co. Sligo, where they were chiefs in two areas, Ó hEaghra Buidhe (fair) around Collooney, and Ó hEaghra Riabhach (grey) at Ballyharry, more properly 'Ballyhara'. In the fourteenth century a branch of the family migrated north to the Glens of Antrim and established themselves in the area around the modern town of Ballymena. There they intermarried with powerful local families and acquired great prominence themselves. Another branch, in Sligo, acquired the title Barons Tyrawley in the early eighteenth century and became powerful landlords in counties Sligo and Leitrim.

In some parts of Ulster, notably Fermanagh, O'Hara has been used as a variant of Haren, a name derived from Ó hÁráin, who were prominent in medieval times in the area of Ballymactaggart in that county.

Apart from Dublin, Sligo and Antrim are still the two regions where the surname is most concentrated.

DEMOGRAPHIC DATA

TRADITIONAL FAMILY AREAS
Fermanagh, Sligo

FAMILY RANKING
1890: 206th *1996*: 211th

NO. OF BIRTHS
1890: 110

Famous Names

WILLIAM O'HARA (1816–1899)

The first Roman Catholic bishop of Scranton, Pennsylvania in the USA.

JOHN O'HARA (1905–1970)

An American writer of novels and short stories, celebrated in his day. His novel *Ten North Frederick* (1955) won the National Book Award, and the Rodgers and Hart musical *Pal Joey* (1940) was based on a short story of his.

FRANK O'HARA (1923–1968)

Another O'Hara winner of the National Book Award. The award was for his *Collected Poems*, published posthumously in 1970.

MAUREEN O'HARA (b. 1921)

The stage name of Irish actress Maureen Fitzsimons, best known for such films as *The Quiet Man* (1952) and *Miracle on 34th Street* (1947).

O'Keeffe

HERALDIC BLAZON

Vert a lion rampant or, in chief two dexter hands couped at the wrist erect and apaumée of the last

The names O'Keeffe, and Keeffe, are the anglicised versions of the Irish Ó Caoimh, from *caomh*, meaning 'kind' or 'gentle'. The original Caomh from whom the family descend lived in the early eleventh century, and was a descendant of Art, King of Munster from 742 to 762. For all of their history the family have been strongly associated with Co. Cork. Originally the territory of the family lay along the banks of the Blackwater River, near modern Fermoy, and were active in the wars of the twelfth century between the O'Connors and the Eoghanacht dynasties of Munster. But the arrival of the Normans displaced them, like so many others, and they moved west into the barony of Duhallow, where their territory became known, and is still known, as Pobal O'Keeffe, and where the senior branch of the family had their seat at Dromagh in Dromtarriff parish. The last chiefs of this branch were Domhnall O'Keeffe of Dromagh (d. c. 1655), who was prominent in the Catholic Rebellion of the 1640s, and his son Captain Daniel O'Keeffe, who was killed fighting for King James at the Battle of Aughrim in 1691. The family estates were confiscated and sold in 1703 to the Hollow Blades Company. Even today, Pobal O'Keeffe is still the area in which the name is most common, with surrounding areas of Co. Cork also including many of the name. It remains relatively rare outside that county.

In 1890 more than two-thirds of the births of the name are recorded in Co. Cork.

DEMOGRAPHIC DATA

TRADITIONAL FAMILY AREAS
Cork

FAMILY RANKING
1890: 94th   *1996*: 82nd

NO. OF BIRTHS
1890: 193

Famous Names

THE CONTINENTAL O'KEEFFES

Like many of the dispossessed Irish nobility, the O'Keeffes were active in the service of the Catholic monarchs of Europe. In 1740 Constantine O'Keeffe (b. c. 1670) was admitted to the French aristocracy on the basis of his Irish pedigree, and his long service. The name 'Cuif', found in the Champagne district of northern France, is that of descendants of O'Keeffe soldiers.

DANIEL O'KEEFFE (1740–1786)

A well-known artist in Dublin and London.

JOHN O'KEEFFE (1747–1833)

Daniel O'Keeffe's younger brother, who was a prolific and talented comic dramatist and songwriter.

'DANNO' O'KEEFFE (b. 1907)

The first footballer to win seven All-Ireland medals, as goalkeeper for Kerry for more than eighteen years.

PADRAIG O'KEEFFE (1889–1963)

A renowned traditional musician and traveling fiddle master.

O'Leary

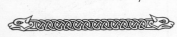

Leary and O'Leary derive from the original Irish Ó Laoghaire, from *laoghaire*, 'a keeper of calves'. Although there was a fifth-century king who gave his name to Dún Laoghaire, the port south of Dublin, no connection exists with the surname, which originated in Co. Cork and is still found predominantly in that area today.

There were originally two families of the name in Cork. The Uí Laoghaire of Dún Cruadha (now Castletownroche) were ousted by the Normans and are not heard of again. The second family originally inhabited the coastal area of south-west Cork, between Roscarbery and Glandore, and according to the traditional genealogies, shared their ancestry with the O'Driscolls. It appears that the Normans displaced them too; at any rate, they migrated to the mountains of Iveleary which now incorporates their name, and became particularly associated with the district of Inchigeelagh. The last chief of the family died in Millstreet, Co. Cork in 1783; like many dispossessed native Irish leaders, he upheld the old traditions of hospitality and patronage and received the respect of the people in return.

One of the most famous poems in Irish literature is *Caoineadh Airt Uí Laoghaire*, the Lament for Art O'Leary, a passionate outpouring of grief and anger written by his widow, Eibhlín Dubh Ní Chonaill (also an aunt of Daniel O'Connell), after his death at the hands of Abraham Morris, one of the local Protestant gentry.

There has been an almost total resumption of the 'O' prefix. Whereas 25% were recorded as 'O'Leary' in 1890, by 1996 the figure was over 99%.

DEMOGRAPHIC DATA

TRADITIONAL FAMILY AREAS
Cork

FAMILY RANKING
1890: 58th   *1996*: 60th

NO. OF BIRTHS
1890:250

Famous Names

JOHN O'LEARY (1830–1907)

A Fenian who in later life became a symbol of the continuity of the nationalist cause. W. B. Yeats used his name in his poem *September 1913*: 'Romantic Ireland's dead and gone / It's with O'Leary in the grave.'

AN T-ATHAIR PEADAR Ó LAOGHAIRE (1839–1920)

An activist in the Gaelic League who saw the need for popular reading matter in Irish and produced it. Two of his works, *Séadna* (1894–97) and *Mo Scéal Féin* (1915) are familiar to anyone who was educated in Ireland between 1930 and 1980.

LIAM O'LEARY (1910–1992)

The man who single-handedly preserved Ireland's cinematic heritage. The Liam O'Leary Film Archive is now in the National Library of Ireland.

DAVE O'LEARY (b. 1958)

A stalwart of the Arsenal FC defence in the English League for almost twenty years, he also played sixty-seven times for the Irish soccer team, scoring the winning penalty against Romania in the 1990 World Cup.

O'Mahony

HERALDIC BLAZON

Quarterly 1st and 4th, a lion rampant azure; 2nd per pale argent and gules a lion rampant counter-changed; 4th, Argent a chevron gules between three snakes tongued proper.

The most common contemporary form of the name O'Mahony, comes from the Irish Ó Mathghamhna, stemming, like MacMahon, from *mathghamhan*, meaning 'bear'. The surname was adopted in the eleventh century by one of the dominant families of the Munster Eoghancht peoples, the Cenel Aeda, whose name is preserved in the barony of Kinalea; the individual from whom the name derives was the child of a marriage between Cian, chief of the Cenel Aeda, and Sadhbh, daughter of Brian Ború. Mathghamhan was a name more commonly associated with the Dál gCais, the sept or tribe of Brian Ború. With the rise of the MacCarthys in the twelfth century, the influence of the O'Mahonys declined, and was largely confined to the area of west Cork with which they are still most strongly associated, the Iveagh peninsula. In this area, perhaps because of its remoteness, they retained a large measure of power and wealth until the final collapse of Gaelic power in the wars of the seventeenth century. According to the account of Sir Richard Cox, writing in that century, there were at least twelve O'Mahony castles in the area. Their ruins can still be seen at Dunbecon, Dunmanus, Three Castle Island and Leamcon, amongst others. In addition, minor branches of the family – minor purely in terms of seniority – were created in Muskerry and Kinalmeaky baronies in Co. Cork, in particular the area around the modern town of Bandon.

Famous Names

COUNT DANIEL O'MAHONY (d. 1714)

The best known of the family to fight in the European armies of the eighteenth century, the 'hero of Cremona'.

COLONEL JOHN O'MAHONY (1815–1877)

Scholar, soldier and revolutionary, he was a founder of the Fenian Brotherhood in the USA, as well as leader of the 99th Regiment of the New York National Guard in the American Civil War and a translator of some distinction.

FRANCIS SYLVESTER MAHONY (1804–1866)

Better known under his pen-name of Father Prout, he was the composer of one of the most famous ballads celebrating Cork city, *The Bells of Shandon*.

EOIN ('THE POPE') O'MAHONY (1904–1970)

The most famous modern bearer of the name was a barrister, lecturer, writer and genealogist, who preserved and interpreted with accuracy and enthusiasm the traditions of his own and many other families, founding and organizing the annual clan gathering of the O'Mahonys.

O'Neill

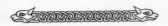

In Irish O'Neill is Ó Néill, from the personal name Niall, possibly meaning 'passionate'. The O'Neill family should not be confused with the Uí Néill, the powerful tribal group claiming descent from the fifth century monarch Niall of the Nine Hostages. Out of the Uí Néill came other well-known surnames, such as O'Doherty, O'Hagan and O'Donnell. Within the Uí Néill, the two main sub-groups were the Cenél Eoghain and the Cenél Conaill, claiming descent from Eoghan and Conall, two of Niall's sons. The O'Neills were the leading family of the Cenél Eoghain, ruling the territory of Tir Eoghain, including modern Tyrone and large parts of Derry and Donegal. The first to use the name in recognisable hereditary fashion was Donal, (b. c. 943) basing his name on Niall Glun Dubh, High King of Ireland (d. 919).

In the fourteenth century a branch of the Tir Eoghain O'Neills migrated east and, led by Aodh Buidhe (Yellow Hugh), wrested much of Antrim and Down from Norman control. The territory at the centre of their power, Clandeboy, took its name from them and they in turn became known as the Clandeboye O'Neills. Their principal castle was at Edenduffcarrig, north-west of Antrim town, still occupied by an O'Neill. This branch's present titular head is Hugo O'Neill, O'Neill of Clandeboy, a Portuguese businessman descended from Muircheartach, chief of the family from 1548 to 1552. The Tyrone family descent also continued unbroken to the present holder of the title Ó Néill Mor, Don Carlos O'Neill of Seville. He is descended, through the O'Neills of the Fews in Co. Armagh, from Aodh, second son of Eoghan, inaugurated as Chief of the Name in 1432.

DEMOGRAPHIC DATA

TRADITIONAL FAMILY AREAS
Antrim, Derry, Down, Tyrone

FAMILY RANKING
1890: 19th   *1996*: 10th

NO. OF BIRTHS
1890: 407

Famous Names

EUGENE O'NEILL (1888–1953)

This dramatist and winner of the 1936 Nobel Prize for Literature, was the son of an emigrant from Co. Kilkenny. Conflicts with his family and cultural heritage formed the basis of much of his work.

FRANCIS O'NEILL (1848–1936)

Superintendent of the Chicago Police but originally from Bantry, Francis O'Neill is renowned in traditional music circles for the enormous collection of melodies he published in his 1903 *Music of Ireland – 1850 Melodies: Airs, Jigs, Reels, Hornpipes, Long Dances, Marches etc.*

TERENCE O'NEILL (1912–90)

Prime Minister of Northern Ireland from 1963 until his resignation in 1969. His efforts at reform failed to prevent the violence which has continued up to the present.

O'Reilly

Reilly, with its variants Riley and (O')R(e)ily, comes from the Irish Ó Raghallaigh, 'grandson of Raghallach' thought to be from *ragh* meaning 'race' and *ceallach*, 'sociable'. The family were part of the Connachta tribal grouping and the Raghallach from whom the name is derived is said to have been a descendant of the O'Conor kings of Connacht. He died at the Battle of Clontarf in 1014.

The name is extremely common and widespread throughout Ireland. Its origin is in the old kingdom of Breffny, which included areas now in counties Cavan and Longford, where the O'Reillys were long the dominant family, despite many attempts by their main rivals, the O'Rourkes, to make it otherwise. The inauguration place of the family was the hill of Shantemon in Castleterra parish. They were renowned in medieval Ireland for their involvement in trade; their success may be gauged by the fact the 'reilly' was at one point a colloquial term for money in Ireland. What use they made of their prosperity can only be conjectured, but the phrase 'the life of Reilly' is suggestive.

After the collapse of Gaelic power in the seventeenth century, large numbers emigrated to serve in the armies of France, many in Colonel Edmund O'Reilly's regiment of foot. The connection with the original homeland is still strong, however; even today (O')Reilly is the single most numerous surname in both Cavan and Longford.

The return of the prefix has been spectacular. Less than 10% give their name as 'O'Reilly' in 1890, but almost 60% in 1996.

TRADITIONAL FAMILY AREAS
Cavan, Longford

FAMILY RANKING
1890: 8th   *1996*: 11th

NO. OF BIRTHS
1890: 586

Famous Names

COUNT ALEXANDER O'REILLY (1722–1794)

Born in Co. Meath, he fought in the armies of Spain where he became governor of Madrid and Cadiz, and captain-general of Andalucia. His later career took him to Cuba, where many O'Reillys are still to be found. His name is recorded in Calle Orely in Havana.

JOHN BOYLE O'REILLY (1844–1890)

Also Co. Meath-born. After transportation to Australia for membership of the Fenians, he escaped and made his way to the US in 1869, where he became proprietor of the *Boston Pilot*.

A. J. F. (TONY) O'REILLY (b. 1936)

The best-known contemporary bearer of the name. Continuing the trading tradition of the family, he is president and chief executive of the Heinz Corporation, as well as having extensive personal business interests worldwide, including effective control of most Irish national newspapers. He played international rugby for Ireland for sixteen years from 1955 to 1970, winning twenty-nine caps.

O'Riordan

HERALDIC BLAZON

Quarterly 1st and 4th, Gules out f the clouds in the sinister side a dexter arm fessways proper holding a dagger in pale argent pommel and hilt or; 2nd and 3rd, Argent a lion rampant gules against a tree in the dexter couped proper.

Riordan, with its variants O'Riordan and Reardan, comes from the Irish original Ó Rioghbhardáin (Riordáin in modern Irish), *riogh-*, 'royal', and *bardán*, a diminutive of bard, 'poet'. The surname originated in the area known as 'Ely O'Carroll', the kingdom of Éile, between the modern towns of Thurles in Co. Tipperary and Birr in Co. Offaly. With the rise of the O'Briens in the tenth and eleventh centuries, this kingdom was fragmented and by the twelfth century, the Ó Rioghbhardain are recorded further south, in Co. Cork. Their migration may have taken them through east Cork, where the townland of Ballyreardon bears their name but by the fifteenth and sixteenth centuries they were securely settled in the west of the county, in Muskerry particularly, where they were faithful followers of the MacCarthys. With the MacCarthys, they were active in the rebellions of the late sixteenth century and at the Battle of Kinsale in 1602; after that defeat many sailed away with the Spaniards, and numerous O'Riordans are later recorded in the Spanish army in Flanders. The family were also active in the Jacobite cause later in the century. Daniel O'Riordan, a captain in Dillon's Regiment in the French army, obtained admission to the French nobility in 1700 and the family are still well known in the areas around Nantes.

The resumption of the 'O' prefix by the family has been remarkable: whereas 94% of births of the name in 1890 are for 'Riordan', by 1996 almost 70% of households are 'O'Riordan'.

TRADITIONAL FAMILY AREAS
Cork

FAMILY RANKING
1890: 122nd *1996*: 112th

NO. OF BIRTHS
1890: 159

Famous Names

SEAN P. Ó RIORDÁIN (1905–1957)

Sean P. Ó Riordáin, born in Monkstown, Co. Cork, was one of the most important archaeologists of his generation, becoming professor of Archaeology in University College Cork in 1936, and professor of Celtic Archaeology in University College Dublin in 1943.

SEAN Ó RIORDÁIN (1916–1971)

Born in Ballyvourney, Co. Cork, he spent most of his life in Cork city as an official of Cork Corporation. Even before the publication of his first book of poems, *Eireaball Spideoige* in 1952, his unique talent was widely recognised and he is now considered by many to have been the finest Irish-language poet of the twentieth century.

O'Shea

HERALDIC BLAZON
Per bend indented azure
and or two fleur-de-lis
counterchanged

The names O'Shea, Shea and (O')Shee are anglicisations of the Irish Ó Seaghdha, from the personal name Seaghdha, meaning either 'hawk-like' or 'fortunate'. The surname arose in south Kerry, on the Iveragh peninsula, where the family held power in the early Middle Ages. Despite the later decline in their influence, they were not displaced, and remained numerous in their homeland up to the present day. Many of the name (usually found as 'Shee' or 'O'Shee') were also prominent in the armies of European Catholic monarchs after the final defeat of Gaelic Ireland in the seventeenth century.

The surname is also found, as Shee and O'Shee, in some numbers in counties Tipperary and Kilkenny. These are the descendants of family members who migrated north as early as the fourteenth century. They became prominent in Kilkenny especially, where the name was more often anglicised (O')Shee and they were one of the so-called 'Ten Tribes of Kilkenny'. The family is now known as the Poer O'Shees. The townland of Sheestown in that county records their influence.

The most famous bearer of the name in Irish history was Katherine ('Kitty') O'Shea, mistress and later wife of the great political leader Charles Stewart Parnell; the disclosure of their love affair brought about Parnell's downfall and changed the course of Irish history.

The resumption of the 'O" prefix, at least within Ireland, has been truly remarkable: from less than 16% of families in 1890 to over 97% in 1996.

Famous Names

SIR MARTIN ARCHER SHEE (1769–1850)

President of the Royal Irish Academy for almost twenty years.

JACK O'SHEA (b. 1957) AND PAUDIE O'SHEA (b. 1955)

Jack and Paudie O'Shea are two of the best Gaelic footballers the country
has known, winning between them fifteen All-Ireland medals with the
Kerry team between 1975 and 1986.

JOHN O'SHEA (b. 1944)

The founder and director of the Third World development and relief
agency GOAL. His passionate commitment to his beliefs has made him
a national figure.

O'Sullivan

The original Irish is Ó Suileabháin, deriving from *súil* (eye), but the meaning of the second part of the name is disputed, leaving the alternatives 'one-eyed' or 'hawk-eyed'. Another option, proposed by Diarmuid Ó Murchadha, gives their ancestor as Súildubán (dark-eyed), chief of a branch of the Munster Eoganachta tribal group, descended, along with such prominent families as the MacCarthys and O'Callaghans, from the mythical Eoghan, supposedly one of the original Gaelic invaders. But historically their exact descent is more difficult to trace. According to some accounts, they were originally based in south Tipperary, around Knockgraffon, but by the start of the thirteenth century were firmly established in the areas with which they are still associated, in the south and west of modern Cork and Kerry. The move was almost certainly the result of encroachments by the O'Briens and the Norman invaders.

By the end of the fourteenth century the family had split into at least seven groupings. The most important were the Clann Gilla Mochuda of south Kerry, who in the sixteenth century changed their surname completely to McGillycuddy, the O'Sullivan Mór, based on the shores of Kenmare Bay, and the O'Sullivan Beare, rulers of the area around Bantry and of the Beara peninsula in Co. Cork.

248

Famous Names

JOHN L. SULLIVAN (1858–1918)

The Boston-born son of emigrants from Tralee, he became one of the most famous boxers in history.

SEÁN O'SULLIVAN (1906–1964)

A distinguished portrait artist and designer.

MAUREEN O'SULLIVAN (b. 1911)

Originally from Boyle, Co. Roscommon, Maureen O'Sullivan had a long career in Hollywood playing, among many other roles, Jane to Johnny Weismuller's Tarzan. She is the mother of the actress Mia Farrow.

SONIA O'SULLIVAN (b. 1967)

One of the most remarkable athletes Ireland has ever produced. Despite repeated disappointment at Olympic level, she has held numerous world records for middle-distance running.

O'Toole

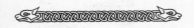

HERALDIC BLAZON
Gules a lion passant
argent

Along with Toole, O'Toole comes from the Irish Ó Tuathail, from the personal name Tuathal, 'ruler of the people'; used by many Irish kings and heroes , it was incorporated into a surname in a number of distinct areas, including south Ulster, Mayo and Kildare. Most bearers of the name today are descended from the Kildare O'Tooles. The individual from whom the surname is taken was Tuathal, King of Leinster (d. c. 958); the first to use the surname in hereditary fashion appears to have been his grandson Doncaon, slain at Leighlin in 1014.

Although the original territory of the O'Tooles lay in Co. Kildare, in the twelfth century they were displaced by the invading Normans, and migrated into adjoining Wicklow, where the area they controlled was roughly identical to the old diocese of Glendalough, with the centre of their power in the region around the Glen of Imaal. Despite the proximity of Dublin and the English administration, the O'Tooles remained fiercely independent and, with their neighbours and occasional allies the O'Byrnes, were a source of great fear to the inhabitants of Dublin and the Pale for almost four centuries. It was only in the seventeenth century, with the final collapse of Gaelic power, that the O'Tooles were 'pacified'.

Unlike most of the Gaelic aristocracy, however, the O'Toole line survived intact; there were two branches, of Powerscourt and Castle Kevin, both in Wicklow. Descendants of the former are living in Wicklow and in the USA. The representatives of the latter have lived in France for many generations.

DEMOGRAPHIC DATA

TRADITIONAL FAMILY AREAS
Kildare, Mayo

FAMILY RANKING
1890: 153rd *1996*: 130th

NO. OF BIRTHS
1890: 139

Famous Names

ST LAURENCE O'TOOLE (1132–1180)

Undoubtedly the most famous bearer of the name is this member of the leading O'Toole family who became abbot of the monastery of Glendalough at the age of twenty-five. He was chosen by the people and clergy as first archbishop of Dublin in 1162 and subsequently led the resistance and negotiation with the Norman invaders.

THE O'TOOLES OF LIMOGES

From Captain Lauence O'Toole of Wexford, an officer in the Irish Brigade of the French army are descended the family of Count O'Toole of Limoges.

PETER O'TOOLE (b. 1932)

Born in Connemara and brought up in England, actor Peter O'Toole has received seven Oscar nominations for his film roles. The best known of these is probably in the title role of *Lawrence of Arabia* (1962).

Power

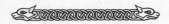

HERALDIC BLAZON
Argent a chief
indented sable

Power is originally a Norman name, which may derive from the Old French *povre*, meaning 'poor', more likely to have referred to a vow than to involuntary destitution; or from *pohier*, meaning 'a native of (the town of) Pois' in Picardy in France, so-called from the Old French *pois*, meaning 'fish', a name given it because of its rivers. The surname is also found in Ireland as 'Le Poer', and in the Irish version 'de Paor'.

The first Norman settlers of name were in Co. Waterford, where Sir Robert Power was granted Lismore by Henry II; members of this family also appear to have been responsible for the original Powerscourt House at Enniskerry in Co. Wicklow, now destroyed. Bearers of the surname Power or le Poer have been earl of Tyrone, marquis of Waterford, counts de la Poer Beresford. It is with Waterford that the surname is most strongly associated – it is the single most numerous surname in the county – although it has also spread into the adjoining counties of Kilkenny, Cork, Tipperary and Wexford. The family which founded Power's distillery, famous for its whiskey, were from Wexford, with their seat at Edermine near Enniscorthy.

This was also the distillery first responsible for the miniature bottle of whiskey, the 'Baby Power', beloved of cold-sufferers throughout Ireland. Its introduction in the 1870s required a special Act of Parliament.

DEMOGRAPHIC DATA

TRADITIONAL FAMILY AREAS
Cork, Kilkenny, Tipperary,
Waterford, Wexford

FAMILY RANKING
1890: 50th *1996*: 43rd

NO. OF BIRTHS
1890: 272

Famous Names

WILLIAM GRATTAN TYRONE POWER (1794–1841)

A celebrated actor, comedian and playwright.

ALBERT POWER (1883–1945)

A sculptor best known for his scuptures of famous subjects and for his memorial to the Lusitania, sunk off Cobh, Co. Cork, in 1915.

ARTHUR POWER (1891–1984)

Best known now for his friendship with James Joyce (he published *Conversations with James Joyce* in 1974), but was a good painter in his own right and helped to introduce modernism to Ireland .

TYRONE POWER (1914–1956)

The great-grandson of William Grattan Tyrone Power was also an actor, who swashbuckled his way through many Hollywood classics.

RICHARD POWER (1928–1970)

A novelist and civil servant, Richard Power's best works are *The Land of Youth* (1966) and *The Hungry Grass* (1969).

Quigley

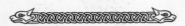

HERALDIC BLAZON
Gules an orle argent,
over all a bend erminois

Quigley is the principal English version of the Irish Ó Coigligh, from *coigleach*, meaning 'unkempt'. Other versions include the rare O'Quigley, Kegley, Twigley and, in parts of Co. Down, Fivey, derived from a mistaken association with the Irish for five, *cúig*. The main origin of the family was in Co. Mayo, in the barony of Carra, near the modern town of Westport, where they were part of the powerful Uí Fiachriagh tribal grouping. From there they were dispersed at an early date, principally to the adjacent territories now part of counties Sligo, Donegal and Derry, where the name is principally found today. The surname also appears to have arisen separately in Inishowen in Donegal, and members of this family have been prominent churchmen in Fermanagh and Monaghan.

There appears also to have been a separate Ó Coigligh family which arose in Co. Wexford, where the name has been anglicised for the most part as Cogley, although Quigley is also frequent.

TRADITIONAL FAMILY AREAS
Derry, Donegal, Mayo, Sligo

FAMILY RANKING
1890: 264th   *1996*: 253rd

NO. OF BIRTHS
1890: 89

Famous Names

DR JAMES EDWARD QUIGLEY (d. 1915)

Bishop of Buffalo in New York State, and a prominent supporter of the
trade union movement.

JOE QUIGLEY (1919–1993)

As surgeon of the Garda Síochána, the Irish police force, from 1958 to
1984, Joe Quigley oversaw the medical aspects of the modernisation of
the force with compassion and thoroughness.

SIR GEORGE QUIGLEY (b. 1929)

One of Northern Ireland's top civil servants and now chairman of Ulster
Bank and a director of National Westminster Bank.

MITCHEL V. COGLEY (1910–1991)

A very well known and respected sports journalist, and sports editor of
the *Irish Independent* for twenty-two years, with a legendary versatility in
the range of sports he was familiar with.

Quinn

HERALDIC BLAZON
Vert a pegasus passant
wings elevated argent,
a chief or

Quinn is now one of the most numerous of Irish surnames, and is to be found in every county in Ireland. The name arose separately in five distinct areas. In four of these – near the modern town of Corofin in Co. Clare, in the glens of north Antrim, near Castlebar in Co. Mayo and in Co. Longford – the Irish original from which the surname derives is Ó Cuinn, from Conn, a popular personal name meaning 'chief' or 'leader'. The family based in Clare were very prominent – the barony of Inchiquin bears their name. The first to use name was Niall Ó Cuinn, who fought and died in the army of Brian Ború at the Battle of Clontarf in 1014. In early times they were chiefs of the Clan Heffernan, and their descendants are today Earls of Dunraven and Mountearl. Their seat was Adare Manor in Co. Limerick, now a hotel and golf course. The seventh earl still lives nearby.

The fifth area where the name originated is Tyrone; today Quinn is the most common surname in the county. The family were part of the Clann Feargusa, descendants of Fergus, grandson of Niall of the Nine Hostages, the fifth-century monarch who founded the dynasty of the Uí Néill. The individual from whom descent is claimed was Coínne, a grandson of Fergus. All of the Clann Feargusa were conspicuous in the fighting forces of the O'Neills, with the Ó Coinne traditionally acting as quartermasters.

DEMOGRAPHIC DATA

TRADITIONAL FAMILY AREAS
Antrim, Clare, Longford, Limerick,
Mayo, Tyrone

FAMILY RANKING
1890: 18th   *1996*: 17th

NO. OF BIRTHS
1890: 406

Famous Names

EDEL QUINN (1907–1944)

A missionary of the Legion of Mary in Africa, working in Kenya,
Mauritius, Uganda and the then Tanganyika and Nyasaland, and
renowned for her dedication in the face of poor health.

FEARGAL QUINN (b. 1936)

The owner of a supermarket chain and a national figure in Ireland due to
his public service and his membership of the Senate, to which he was
elected in 1993.

RUARÍ QUINN (b. 1946)

Ruarí Quinn is presently deputy leader of the Labour Party. He has
served in five ministries, including his role as minister for Finance.

AIDAN QUINN (b. 1959)

A native of Belfast who is well known as a Hollywood actor, having
appeared in such films as *Desperately Seeking Susan* (1985), *The Mission*
(1986) and *Legends of the Fall* (1994).

Redmond

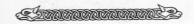

HERALDIC BLAZON

Gules a castle with two towers argent between three woolpacks or

Redmond is a Norman surname, derived from the personal name Raymond or Raimund, made up of the Germanic roots *ragin*, 'counsel', and *mund*, 'protection'. The first of the name in Ireland was Alexander Redmond (or FitzRedmond), who was granted the Hook area of Co. Wexford in the first wave of Norman settlers. His descendants Robert and Walter built Redmond's Hall in the early fourteenth century, and the family became known as the Redmonds of the Hook and the Hall. The descent of the senior lines is well documented down to the twentieth century, although they were dispossessed of much of their property, including Redmond's Hall, in the seventeenth century. It is now known as Loftus Hall, after the grantee, Nicholas Loftus. Other lines of the family, descended from younger sons, flourished and multiplied to the point where Redmond is now an extremely common name throughout Co. Wexford. Other branches have also established themselves throughout Ireland.

A native Irish family of Co. Wexford, the MacDavymores, also adopted the Redmond name in the early seventeenth century, taking it from their fourteenth century ancestor, Redmond MacDavymore. This family were descended from Murchadh na nGael, brother of Dermot MacMurrough, the king of Leinster whose alliance with the Normans resulted in their invasion. Their adoption of the surname seems to have been an attempt to retain their lands by association with the Anglo-Irish family of the name. In any case, they were based in the north of the county, while the Norman Redmonds are most strongly associated with south Wexford, where they first settled.

DEMOGRAPHIC DATA

TRADITIONAL FAMILY AREAS
Wexford

FAMILY RANKING
1890: 295th   *1996*: 284th

NO. OF BIRTHS
1890: 79

Famous Names

JOHN EDWARD REDMOND (1855–1918)

The most famous bearer of the name and leader of the Irish
Parliamentary Party in the British House of Commons until the party
was eclipsed by the rise of Sinn Féin.

THE REDMOND POLITICIANS

The immediate family of John Redmond, which claimed descent from
the old Norman stock, was remarkable for the number of politicians it
produced; no fewer than seven others became MPs in the UK parliament
or TDs in the Irish Dáil after independence.

Regan

HERALDIC BLAZON
Or a chevron ermine
between three dolphins
azure

Regan, along with its variants Reagan and O'Re(a)gan, comes from the Irish Ó Riagáin, perhaps from *riodhgach*, meaning 'impulsive' or 'angry'. It originated independently in at least three different areas.

In the Meath/Dublin region it was borne by one of the Four Tribes of Tara, prominent in the wars with the Vikings. After the Norman invasion they were dispossessed, and migrated westwards to the area now part of Co. Laois, where their descendants are still to be found. A second family claims descent from Riagan, a nephew of the eleventh-century High King Brian Ború; their homeland was the historic kingdom of Thomond, in an area now covered by parts of Co. Limerick.

East Cork, around the modern town of Fermoy, was the original territory of the third family of Ó Riagáin. Their influence in the wider area of east Cork is recorded in the townland names of Coolyregan in Brigown parish, and two Ballyregans, in the parishes of Cloyne and Carrigtohill. Like many other native families, however, they were driven out by the Normans and their allies and by the sixteenth century, most members of this family had migrated to the south-west, and it is with west Cork that the name is most strongly linked today. The main seat of the family was at Ballinaclogh, in the civil parish of Ross.

There would also appear to have been one more family of the name, based in Connacht, where the surname is today still numerous in counties Mayo and Roscommon.

TRADITIONAL FAMILY AREAS
Cork, Limerick, Laois, Mayo,
Roscommon

FAMILY RANKING
1890: 70th *1996*: 122nd

NO. OF BIRTHS
1890: 219

Famous Names

SIR TEIGE MAC SHANE O REGAN (1629–c. 1698)

The last chief of the name of the west Cork family. He was an officer in
the Jacobite army in 1690 and for his part in the defence of Charlemont
fort in Co. Armagh was knighted by King James. After the Battle of the
Boyne he became governor of Sligo and in 1691 left for the Continent
with the rest of the defeated army. The O'Regan lands at Ballinaclogh
remained in the family until the early twentieth century.

RONALD REAGAN (b. 1911)

Fortieth president of the USA, was also of the Cork O'Regans, though
his ancestors were among those who were not displaced from east to west
Cork. Before becoming president he had a long career as a broadcaster
and film actor and was governor of California from 1967 to 1974.

Roche

HERALDIC BLAZON
Gules three roaches
naiant in pale argent

Roche, together with its variants Roach, Roch, etc., is a name of Norman origin. Although the obvious derivation is from the French *roche*, 'rock', the earliest bearer of the surname in Ireland, Richard FitzGodebert de la Roche, in fact adopted the surname after his place of origin in Wales, Rhos in Pembrokeshire. He was one of the first Norman arrivals, coming in 1167, and acquiring with others of his family large tracts of south Co. Wexford. Over the centuries the family became thoroughly hibernicised, to the point where they were prominent in the many rebellions against English rule, the best-known being Father Philip Roche, who led the Irish in the Battle of Horetown in 1798. The name is still strongly linked with Co. Wexford, where six townlands called Rochestown exist today; the family name is also recorded in at least thirty placenames across the country, such as Ballinroche (Limerick), Raheenroche (Kilkenny), Rochfort (Galway), and Castletownroche (Cork). The latter reflects the family's prominence around the modern town of Fermoy in Co. Cork, where they prospered. They became Viscounts Roche, a title which became extinct in the eighteenth century. In 1856 Edmund Burke-Roche of Trabolgan was created Baron Fermoy. The present eighth baronet is Edmund James Burke-Roche.

The name also proliferated further afield and multiplied throughout the southern province of Munster; Roche is today one of the commonest surnames in that area.

There also appears to have been another branch of the family based in the West, where the surname is today common in Co. Mayo.

Famous Names

KEVIN ROCHE (b. 1922)

One of North America's leading architects, celebrated for such designs as the General Foods headquarters and the extensions to the Guggenheim Museum.

BILLY ROCHE (b. 1949)

Billy Roche has worked as a musician and actor but is best known for his plays and novels, which focus on the tensions of small-town life, as represented by his birthplace, Wexford.

ADI ROCHE (b. 1955)

An anti-nuclear campaigner for many years, she is now internationally known for the Chernobyl Children's Project which she set up in 1991 to provide medical treatment and holidays for young victims of the Chernobyl disaster. She was nominated European Person of the Year in 1996.

Rourke

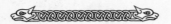

HERALDIC BLAZON
Or two lions passant
in pale sable

With its variants (O')Rorke, Roarke, etc., Rourke comes from the Irish Ó Ruairc, 'grandson of Ruarc'. Ruarc is a personal name from the Old Norse Hrothekr (whence also 'Roderick'), 'famous king'. Viking influence on O'Rourke families is also seen in their use of such first names as Lochlann, Amhlaobh (Olaf) and Sitric.

The O'Rourkes were part of the large tribal grouping of the Ui Briúin, claiming common descent from Brión, a fifth-century king of Connacht, together with such other prominent families as the O'Connors and MacDermotts (Ui Briúin Ai), and the O'Flahertys (Ui Briúin Seola). With the O'Reillys, the O'Rourkes formed the Ui Briúin Breifne. In the early Middle Ages, the O'Connors and the O'Rourkes were engaged in a long struggle for supremacy in Connacht, a struggle which ended in the victory of the O'Connors.

The Ruarc from whom the surname derives was a ninth-century king of Breifne, an area covering most of Leitrim and Cavan, and part of Co. Longford. The first to use his name in a hereditary surname was his grandson, Sean Fearghal O Ruairc (d. 964). For the next century-and-a-half, four O'Rourkes were kings of Connacht, and the family became one of the most powerful in Ireland. After the twelfth century, they appear to have accepted the overlordship of the O'Connors. They also had problems with the other pre-eminent family of Breifne, the O'Reillys, which ultimately resulted in their territory being much reduced. The main stronghold of the family was at Dromahaire, on the shores of Lough Gill in Co. Leitrim.

DEMOGRAPHIC DATA

TRADITIONAL FAMILY AREAS
Cavan, Leitrim

FAMILY RANKING
1890: 157th *1996*: 121st

NO. OF BIRTHS
1890: 136

Famous Names

GENERAL COUNT IOSIF KORNILIEVICH O ROURKE (1772–1849)

This nephew of John O Rourke Prince of Breifne (b. 1735) was one of the Russian generals who defeated Napoleon. Many other members of the family were also prominent in Tsarist Russia.

COUNT EDWARD O ROURKE

Count Edward O Rourke, another member of the family, was bishop of Danzig before the Second World War.

Ryan

HERALDIC BLAZON
Gules three griffins
heads erased argent

Ryan is today one of the commonest surnames in Ireland. The vast majority of Ryans today are descended from the family of Ó Maoilriagháin, meaning 'descendant of a devotee of St. Riaghan'. The anglicisation Mulryan began to fade as early as the seventeenth century, and is today virtually unknown apart from a few pockets in counties Galway and Leitrim, possibly derived from a different family. As Mulryan it has also been recorded in Spain, among the descendants of Irish émigrés. The surname first appears in the fourteenth century in the barony of Owney (formerly Owney O'Mulryan) on the borders of counties Limerick and Tipperary, where the Ó Maoilriagháin displaced the O'Heffernans. Even today the surname is highly concentrated in this area.

In Carlow and adjoining areas, Ryan may also derive from Ó Riagháin, sometimes confused with Regan. From their origin in the barony of Idrone in Carlow (they were chiefs of the Uí Drone) this family spread widely into the adjoining counties of Wexford and Kilkenny. Members of the Ryan family of Tomcoole in Wexford have been prominent in Irish politics for almost a century, over three generations.

The surname was ranked seventh most common in 1890 and sixth in 1996. An educated guess at the total of Ryans in Ireland at present puts their number at something over 28,000.

DEMOGRAPHIC DATA

TRADITIONAL FAMILY AREAS
Carlow, Tipperary

FAMILY RANKING
1890: 7th *1996*: 6th

NO. OF BIRTHS
1890: 715

Famous Names

PATRICK J. RYAN (1883–1964)

An emigrant to the US, he won a gold medal for hammer-throwing for his adopted country in the 1920 Olympics, before returning to farming in Pallasgreen in Limerick. The record he set in 1913 stood for twenty-five years.

JOHN RYAN (1925–1992)

Although he had a long and varied career as a broadcaster, painter, publisher and owner of the famous Bailey pub in Dublin, John Ryan will be remembered best for his association with Flann O'Brien, Patrick Kavanagh and Brendan Behan.

TONY RYAN (b. 1936)

Tony Ryan has had mixed fortunes as one of Ireland's leading businessmen. His aircraft leasing company Guinness Peat Aviation was one of the most successful in the world until its virtual collapse in 1992. With his sons, he now controls Ireland's only independent airline, Ryanair.

RICHARD RYAN (b. 1946)

A distinguished poet and currently Ireland's ambassador to Korea.

Sheehan

HERALDIC BLAZON

Azure on a mount in base
vert a dive argent holding
in the beak an olive
branch prope

Sheehan is the anglicisation of the Irish Ó Siodhacháin, thought to be from a diminutive of *siodhach*, meaning 'peaceful'. The principal family of the name were part of the Dál gCais, the tribal grouping occupying an area now in counties Limerick and Clare which produced Brian Ború, High King of Ireland in the eleventh century. Some of the traditional genealogies have the descent of the Sheehans from one Sidhechan, a contemporary of Brian Ború, and distantly related to him. Initially they appear to have lived in the south of Co. Limerick, in the barony of Connello. In very early times, however, they migrated south, into the north-east of the present Co. Cork, where they are still most numerous. Over the course of the centuries, large numbers have also migrated into Co. Kerry, while a significant number also remained in their homeland of Limerick.

A separate family of Ó Siodhacháin is also recorded in medieval times among the Uí Maine in the Galway/Roscommon region, as hereditary musicians to the O'Kellys, but very few of the name remain in this area. It is with Cork and Kerry that the name is now indelibly associated.

TRADITIONAL FAMILY AREAS
Cork

FAMILY RANKING
1890: 76th   *1996*: 102nd

NO. OF BIRTHS
1890: 215

Famous Names

MICHAEL SHEEHAN (1870–1945)

An archbishop of Sydney who is remembered also for his work on behalf of the last Irish-speaking area of Waterford, Ring.

CANON PATRICK SHEEHAN (1852–1913)

A poet and novelist who was internationally famous in his day for such works as *Luke Delmege* (1901), *Glenanaar* (1905) and *The Graves at Kilnamona* (1915).

Sheridan

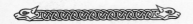

HERALDIC BLAZON

Or a lion rampant
between three
trefoils vert

Sheridan is the English version of Ó Sirideáin, from the personal name Siridean, which is possibly related to *sirim*, meaning 'to seek'. The surname arose in the modern Co. Longford, where the Ó Sirideain held hereditary church offices and land in the parish of Granard. They later moved to the adjoining county of Cavan, where they became followers of the rulers of Breffny, the O'Reillys. Cavan is still the area in which the surname is most common, remaining one of the ten most numerous surnames in the county, though it has now spread throughout the northern half of the country.

The most famous bearer of the name was the playwright Richard Brinsley Sheridan (1751–1817), born in Dublin, whose three masterpieces, *The Rivals*, *The School for Scandal* and *The Critic* display brilliant comic invention. His grandfather Thomas (1687–1738) had been a close friend of the satirist Jonathan Swift and his father, also Thomas (1719–1788), had been an actor and theatre manager in Dublin.

Famous Names

GENERAL PHILIP HENRY SHERIDAN (1831–1888)

Philip Henry Sheridan was born in Killinkere, Co. Cavan but emigrated to the US with his parents. He went on to become a major-general on the Union side in the Civil War, and was later Military Governor of Texas and Louisiana.

RICHARD BINGHAM SHERIDAN (1822–1897)

Born in Castlebar, he emigrated to New South Wales and went on to become a member of the Legislative Assembly and Postmaster General.

JIM SHERIDAN (b. 1949)

A highly successful film director whose film *My Left Foot* (1988) won two Oscars in 1989. He has also won awards for *The Field* (1990) and *In the Name of the Father* (1993).

MARGARET BURKE SHERIDAN (1889–1958)

Called 'the Empress of Ireland' by the conductor Toscanini for her singing. She appeared in many operas at Covent Garden and La Scala.

JOHN D. SHERIDAN (1903–1980)

A hugely popular humourous columnist with the *Irish Independent* newspaper during the 1940s and '50s. In later life he strongly opposed liberal changes in Irish society.

Tobin

HERALDIC BLAZON
Azure three oak
leaves argent

Tobin is in Irish Tóibín, which is a Gaelicised version of the Norman 'de St. Aubin', after the place of the same name in Brittany, so-called from the dedication of its church to St Albin. The family came to Ireland in the immediate aftermath of the Norman invasion, and by the early thirteenth century were well established in counties Kilkenny and Tipperary; their power in the latter county is attested by the (unofficial) title Baron of Coursey by which the head of the family was known in the Middle Ages. In the course of time, the surname also spread into the adjoining counties of Cork and Waterford, and this is the area in which it remains most common by far today.

Placenames including the surname reflect the geographical spread of the family, with Ballytobin and Castletobin in Kilkenny, and Tobinsgarden in Tipperary, and Tobinstown in Carlow.

TRADITIONAL FAMILY AREAS
Kilkenny, Tipperary

FAMILY RANKING
1890: 237th   *1996*: 239th

NO. OF BIRTHS
1890: 98

Famous Names

NIALL TÓIBÍN (b. 1941)

Niall Tóibín is a comic actor celebrated in Ireland for more than thirty years for his gift of mimicry and his mastery of local accents.

COLM TÓIBÍN (b. 1955)

From Enniscorthy, Co. Wexford, Colm Tóibín is one of the country's best-known contemporary novelists, as well as having a successful career in journalism. His most celebrated novel is *The Heather Blazing* (1989).

Walsh

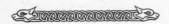

HERALDIC BLAZON

Argent a chevron gules
between three broad arrow
heads points upwards sable

Walsh is among the five most numerous surnames in Ireland, found throughout the country, with particular concentrations in Connacht in counties Mayo and Galway; in Munster in counties Cork and Waterford; and in Leinster in counties Kilkenny and Wexford. It is a semi-translation of the Irish surname Breathnach, meaning 'British' or 'Welsh', also sometimes anglicised as Brannagh. The surname thus has the same historical origin as Wallace, but arrived at its present form by a more circuitous route. Unlike most of the other Hiberno–Norman families, such as the Fitzgeralds, the Burkes, etc., who can trace their ancestry to a small number of known individuals, the Walshes have many different origins, since the name arose independently in many different places, for obvious reasons. Two exceptions should perhaps be mentioned: the descendants of Haylen Brenach, one of those who arrived in 1172, became very well known and prosperous in the south and east of the country, while Walynus, who arrived in 1169, is said to have been the progenitor of the Walshes of Tirawley in Co. Mayo, and the brother of Barrett, the ancestor of the Barretts of the same county.

There are many placenames which record the surname, including at least twelve places called Walshestown.

The variant Welsh is particularly noted in Co. Antrim.

DEMOGRAPHIC DATA

TRADITIONAL FAMILY AREAS
Cork, Galway, Kilkenny, Mayo,
Waterford, Wexford

FAMILY RANKING
1890: 3rd   *1996*: 3rd

NO. OF BIRTHS
1890: 932

Famous Names

ANTOINE VINCENT WALSH (1703–1765)

This son of an Irish émigré to France was captain of the ship which landed the Young Pretender, Prince Charles Edward Stuart ('Bonnie Prince Charlie') in Scotland in 1745, for which service he was knighted.

JOHN WALSH (1830–1898)

A Co. Kilkenny native and the first Catholic archbishop of Toronto.

WILLIAM WALSH (1841–1921)

Roman Catholic archbishop of Dublin from 1885 to 1921 and the first chancellor of the National University of Ireland.

MAURICE WALSH (1879–1964)

Only began to write seriously in his forties but quickly gained fame. The film *The Quiet Man* is based on his short story of the same name.

THOMAS J. WALSH (1911–1988)

Founder and director of the Wexford Festival Opera.

EDWARD WALSH (b. 1939)

The driving force behind the establishment of Limerick University in 1989, and currently its president.

Whelan

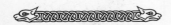

HERALDIC BLAZON

Argent four lozenges in bend conjoined azure between two cotises of the last, on a chief gules three fleur-de-lis of the last

Whelan, along with its common variant Phelan, comes from the Irish Ó Faoláin, from a diminutive of *faol*, 'wolf'. Taken together, the two names come among the fifty most numerous in Ireland. The family originated in the ancient kingdom of Decies, part of the modern county of Waterford, where they were rulers up to the Norman invasion. A minor branch also settled in the adjoining county of Kilkenny. From this centre, the surname has now spread to the adjoining counties of Kilkenny, Cork, Wexford and, further north, Laois and Carlow. It is also to be found throughout the country, however.

Although Whelan is the more common of the two versions, Phelan is the one which has left its mark on Irish placenames, with Kilphelan in Co. Cork and Raheenphelan and Rathphelan both in Co. Laois.

Famous Names

LEO WHELAN (1892–1956)

Leo Whelan was well known as a portrait painter.

SEÁN O'FAOLÁIN (1900–1991)

Born John Francis Whelan in Cork. He was internationally famous in particular for his short stories which present unsparing but compassionate pictures of life in modern Ireland. He was bitterly opposed to the censorship and narrow Catholicism of Ireland in the 1940s and '50s.

JULIA O'FAOLÁIN (b. 1932)

The daughter of Seán O'Faoláin is also a successful novelist and translator.

NUALA O'FAOLÁIN (b. 1942)

Nuala O'Faoláin has had a varied career as a feminist, academic and film-maker, and is best known now for her role as an influential and respected social commentator with the *Irish Times*.

BILL WHELAN (1950–1996)

A composer, songwriter and record producer, best known now for the music he composed for the hugely successful dance show, Riverdance.

Index

COLLINS